Simon Houghton has worked in a number of security related roles in government since 2000. His experience includes formulating departmental security policies, operational delivery of security programmes and auditing compliance of private sector organisations with government security regulations. He has a degree (MA) in Security Management from Loughborough University.

Simon Houghton

An Introduction To Security

ISBN 9781786126931 (Paperback)
ISBN 9781786126948 (Hardback)
ISBN 9781786126955 (eBook)

www.austinmacauley.com

First Published (2016)
Austin Macauley Publishers Ltd.
25 Canada Square
Canary Wharf
London
E14 5LQ

Contents

Introduction

Security is a vital part of any organisation's corporate support. It protects the staff, assets, information and processes the organisation relies on to deliver its business objectives. The study of security is important to managers who have recently taken on security responsibilities within their organisation or students of security related courses who are planning a career as security professionals.

Security is a challenging subject to study as it continually evolves and new concepts are developed which challenge previously held principles and methods. Threats evolve which make accepted security controls obsolete. The application of security models in a practical situation can also be very different from how it functions in theory. Security can be represented more as an art than a science. Science relies on facts derived from testable hypothesis which produce consistent results to form laws and rules. Art builds perspective through creativity, perception and imagination and what is fashionable one moment can be discredited the next. Security requires judgement, adaptability and experience, which is why it is better described as an art.

A textbook analysis of security is not practical with

complete certainty. However, there are broad concepts and principles which have formed a common practice which is recognisable across the security industry. The purpose of this book is to explain such concepts and provide examples of security controls. This will provide the reader with a basic perspective which can be built up through further study and experience.

This book is divided into three sections:

Section 1 - An Overview of Security: describes the main aspects of security, including risk, hazard and asset, and discusses the concept of risk management.

Section 2 - Security Management: describes the methods for managing a security regime, including organising a security team, producing protocols, ensuring compliance with industry standards and legal responsibilities, providing training and equipment and managing the security of contractors.

Section 3 - Security Controls: describes the main concepts of common security fields including physical, personnel, personal, information, IT, communications and document security. It also describes some typical security controls within each field, although, as has already been described, these are not exhaustive.

At the end of this book, the reader will have a basic understanding of the principles of security and how they may operate in practice.

Section 1

An Overview of Security

This section provides an overview of security by examining the concept of risk management and describing its main components. It is broken down as follows:

1.1 **Background:** includes a definition of security and describes the concepts of risk, asset and hazard;

1.2 **Risk Management:** describes risk management and its core components of threat, vulnerability, impact and controls;

1.3 **Risk Assessment:** describes different types of risk assessment and the specific aspects of threat assessment, vulnerability assessment and impact assessment;

1.4 **Risk Mitigation:** describes the four main methods of mitigation - avoidance, transfer, reduction and retention;

1.5 **Risk Assurance:** describes the concepts of monitoring, compliance and reporting; and

1.6 **Risk Review:** describes different types of risk review.

1.1
Background

Security contributes a vital role in helping an organisation meet its legal, moral and business responsibilities which include:

    a. **protecting staff:** assaults and intimidation can dramatically affect staff morale leading to reduced productivity, motivation and competence;

    b. **reducing losses:** attacks against an organisation may cause loss or damage to valuable assets which will require replacing and may also affect the delivery of business objectives;

    c. **maintaining customer and stakeholder confidence:** the organisation may be responsible for looking after assets belonging to another party and the loss or damage to these assets could adversely affect the party's confidence in the organisation;

    d. **fulfilling statutory and regulatory responsibilities:** an organisation has obligations established by law to protect certain assets, such as the personal safety of its staff, and a failure to do so could result in legal liability;

e. **fulfilling contractual obligations:** an organisation may be required to provide goods or services to another party which, if disrupted, could constitute a breach of contract; and

f. **public profile:** the organisation's public image may be important to its work and avoidable security incidents may adversely affect that image.

An effective security regime is critical to an organisation's business and to neglect it is to expose the organisation to serious consequences.

Defining Security

At its broadest interpretation, the word 'security' could include a number of very different subjects, including financial security, social security or international security. In order to define security in relation to the protection of an organisation's assets, the term 'protective security' is often used. However, in the interests of brevity, the word 'security' will be used in isolation throughout this book to refer to 'protective security'.

At its most basic, security can be defined as 'the protection of something valuable from something harmful'. There are specific terms used in the security field to add clarity to this definition. Protection is provided through the management of 'risk', something valuable is known as an 'asset' and something harmful is known as a 'hazard'. A more precise definition of security could, therefore, be 'the management of risk to an asset from a hazard'.

Risk

Risk is the potential consequence of a hazard and can be divided into two categories:

    a.   **static (or pure) risk:** provides the prospect only for loss (e.g. theft or criminal damage); and

    b.   **dynamic (or business) risk:** provides the prospect for both loss and gain. An example is remote working where the risks of having IT systems accessible outside a secure environment could be balanced against the advantages of staff being able to work from home or when travelling on business.

Security has historically focused only on static risk. However, security controls must be proportionate and balance the potential hazard against flexible and efficient working practices. Therefore, a dynamic view of risk must be adopted to ensure security processes consider the gain, as well as the potential loss, involved in business operations.

Asset

An asset is anything of value to the organisation and can be divided into two categories:

a. **tangible assets:** include anything physical, such as staff, buildings, tools, equipment, vehicles, documents or cash; and

b. **intangible assets:** include anything which does not have a physical form or cannot be identified in quantitative terms, such as information, reputation, credibility, customer confidence, intellectual property rights or market share.

Hazard

A hazard is something harmful to an organisation's assets and can be divided into four main categories:

a. **natural:** these occur as a result of normal environmental forces, such as inclement weather and natural disasters;

b. **accidental:** these occur as a result of man-made, but unintentional events such as failure of equipment or utility supplies. They do not necessarily occur without blame, but they do not occur through deliberate intent;

c. **business:** these occur as a result of the organisation's interactions with its partners, clients, customers and competitors and include loss of market share, product failure and legal liability; and

d. **malicious:** these occur as a result of deliberate, unauthorised acts intended to cause harm, such as theft and criminal damage.

Security may have an interest in all these, but its main concern is with malicious hazards which will be the focus of its security regime.

1.2
Risk Management

Risk management is a continual process to ensure risk is controlled to a level the organisation considers to be acceptable. This level is often referred to as the organisation's 'risk appetite'.

There are four stages of risk management:

a. **risk assessment:** to ensure the organisation understands the risks it faces;

b. **risk mitigation:** to establish effective and proportionate security controls to address the risks;

c. **risk assurance:** to monitor and evaluate security controls to ensure they remain effective; and

d. **risk review:** to ensure the assessment, mitigation and assurance stages remain effective and appropriate.

Risk is the interaction between three main factors; the probability (or likelihood) of a hazard occurring, the impact of a hazard and the controls established to mitigate it. Probability is comprised of two factors;

threat (the source of a hazard) and vulnerability (an aspect of an asset that makes it susceptible to a hazard).

The interaction of these factors, and the four stages of risk management, is shown in Figure 1: Risk Management Model.

Fig.1: Risk Management Model

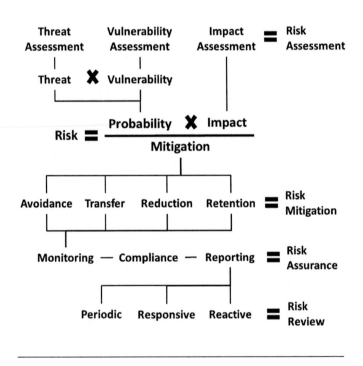

Threat

A threat is the source of a hazard and can include terrorism, crime, corporate espionage, rogue insiders, violent protest and information brokerage. Threat is comprised of three factors:

a. **motive:** the rationale which drives the threat. This can be divided into four categories:
   - generic: the threat considers a number of organisations a potential target and, whilst some may be more desirable than others, has no particular intent towards any one of them and will often pick the easiest target;
   - specific: the threat considers a specific organisation, or group of organisations, to be a valid target;
   - associated: the threat considers the organisation only as a means of gaining access to a greater target it cannot attack directly. For example, the organisation may be a contractor providing services to the desired target and, therefore, may have access to its premises, equipment or information; and
   - collateral: the threat may not consider the organisation a target, but may wish to attack a target associated with it or located close by. The threat may accept the damage its attack will inflict on the organisation.

b. **capability:** the ability of the threat. This includes skills, knowledge, experience, funding and support.

c. **opportunity:** a potential window of attack available to the threat. This is comprised of two factors; time and location. In most cases, an organisation will exist in known premises for a lengthy period of time which will provide a continual opportunity. However, some operations may take place at different locations for a more limited period of time such as the delivery of goods, or external events such as conferences or presentations.

Threat Displacement

An important point in understanding threat is the concept of 'threat displacement'. Threats rarely give up when they meet effective security controls. They adapt to overcome or circumvent the controls and try a different avenue of attack. There are four categories of threat displacement:

a. **target:** the threat can choose a different target altogether. This is the most preferable outcome for the organisation and occurs most commonly when the motive of the threat is generic (ie it has little interest in attacking a specific organisation and is content to pick another in the same area or within the same industry);

b. **territory:** the threat can attack a different part of the organisation in a different location. For instance, if an organisation's main headquarters is well protected, a threat may choose to mount an attack on a small regional office where security is lighter;

c. **tactic:** the threat can adopt a different method of attack. For instance, if physical intrusion to an organisation's premises is impractical, a threat may choose to gain access by applying for a job with the organisation to gain legitimate access to its assets; and

d. **time:** the threat can wait to see if a vulnerability presents itself. The organisation's security may become lax or reduced by budget cuts. Alternatively, the capability of the threat may increase through experience or the availability of greater resources.

Vulnerability

A vulnerability is an aspect of an asset which makes it susceptible to a threat. Vulnerability is comprised of three factors:

a. **weakness:** a feature of an asset which can be exploited in an attack;

b. **exploitable:** how practical the weakness is to exploit; and

c. **known:** how openly the above factors are known or how accurately they could be anticipated.

Impact

The impact is the potential consequence of a hazard on an asset. Impact can be measured both in terms of scale (e.g. the cost and time of recovery) and characteristics (e.g. the unique effect of a hazard on a particular asset or collection of assets). Impacts are often unique to the type of assets, for example:

a. **people:** health, safety or motivation;

b. **property:** damage, loss or sabotage;

c. **facilities:** damage, unauthorised access, availability of services; and

d. **information:** confidentiality, integrity and availability.

Mitigation

Risk mitigation can be divided into four categories:

a. **avoidance:** avoiding the activity which generates the risk. For instance, paying staff by bank transfer avoids the risk of payroll robbery when paying them by cash;

b. **transfer:** moving the risk to another organisation. For instance, contracting out IT services is a method of shifting IT risks to a service provider;

c. **reduction:** reducing either the probability of a risk or its impact by implementing security controls; and

d. **retention:** the risk is not mitigated any further and is retained, either actively or passively.

1.3
Risk Assessment

The previous section highlighted that the aim of risk assessment is to ensure the organisation is aware of, and understands, the risks it faces. Risk assessment is a three stage process, including:

   a. **identification:** to highlight the risks;

   b. **analysis:** to examine how the risks may affect an asset; and

   c. **evaluation:** to determine the extent of the risks.

Qualitative and Quantitative Assessment

There are two types of risk assessment:

   a. **qualitative:** a subjective analysis of risk based on evidence gathered and analysed; and

   b. **quantitative:** an objective analysis of risk based on a calculation using defined values attributed to specific evidence.

The distinction between the two is that the focus of a qualitative assessment is the outcome, the process only supports this; whilst the focus of a quantitative assessment is the process, the outcome is automatically generated from it. No assessment is completely qualitative or quantitative. A qualitative assessment will still require a method and structure and a quantitative assessment will still require some judgement and perspective to understand and interpret the data.

An example of a qualitative assessment is where a panel of individuals from across the organisation discuss risks and agree on an assessment. Their individual skills and experience provides them with a professional perspective to interpret and assess the information and reach a broad consensus on the risk. An example of a quantitative assessment is where evidence is input into a software application which defines the information it requires, attributes a value to it and produces an assessment based on its calculation of this information. There are strengths and limitations to both types of assessment.

Qualitative assessments are often inconsistent. Even if a uniform method or structure is used for each assessment, different individuals will attribute importance to evidence based on their own experiences and prejudices. Even the same individual may reach a different conclusion for the same assessment made at different times. For instance, an assessment in response to a security incident may evaluate the risk to be high whilst an assessment made during a cost cutting exercise may evaluate the risk as much lower. The circumstances behind the risk assessment will influence its outcome and consistency. Quantitative assessments will always use the same set of values and, provided the information input is the same, the evaluation should always be consistent.

Quantitative assessments, especially those which rely on computer programs, are able to process large volumes of complex information, analyse it and produce an assessment quickly. However, the method they use to make such calculations can often be unfathomable to anyone other than those who built the program. Therefore, it is often difficult for organisations to understand whether the assessment has accurately interpreted and analysed all the information which has been input. Qualitative assessments usually have a more transparent methodology which is much easier to scrutinise.

Quantitative assessments can appear more credible and factual than qualitative assessments as they use a uniform method relying on objective data. Qualitative assessments relying on subjective views of participants are often open to argument. Qualitative assessments often take longer than quantitative ones as they often require a greater level of consideration and reflection.

These are very broad descriptions and different risk assessment methods will have their own attributes which may be different from those outlined above. However, this serves to illustrate the general strengths and weaknesses which are commonly found in each method.

Threat Assessment

Threat is the source of a hazard and is comprised of motive, capability and opportunity. Therefore, a threat assessment is an examination of these elements in order to reach an evaluation of the nature and severity of the threat. A threat assessment can be divided into four stages:

a. **identification of the threats:** this usually includes a list of potential threats and a brief description of their relevance to the organisation.

b. **analysis of the components of each threat:** this will be determined by the particular methodology adopted (ie quantitative or qualitative) and will examine the elements of motive, capability and opportunity;

c. **evaluation of the extent of each threat:** this will be driven by the analysis and will usually score each threat on an ascending scale (e.g. negligible, low, moderate, high and severe); and

d. **ordering the threats:** this involves organising the threats into a list to highlight the most serious.

Vulnerability Assessment

Vulnerability is an aspect of an asset which makes it susceptible to a threat and is comprised of a weakness which is exploitable and known. Therefore, a vulnerability assessment is an examination of each of these elements to evaluate the nature and severity of each vulnerability. A vulnerability assessment can be divided into four stages:

a. **identification of the vulnerabilities:** this can be done by examining each potential avenue of attack, usually broken down by security field (e.g. physical, personnel, personal, information and operations security);

b. **analysis of the components of each vulnerability:** this will be determined by the particular methodology adopted (ie quantitative or qualitative) and will examine the elements of weakness, exploitable and known;

c. **evaluation of the extent of each vulnerability:** this will be driven by the analysis and will usually score each vulnerability on an ascending scale (e.g. negligible, low, moderate, high and severe); and

d. **ordering the vulnerabilities:** this involves organising the vulnerabilities into a list to highlight the most serious.

Impact Assessment

Impact of a hazard is unique to the asset it affects. An impact assessment is an examination of the effect of a potential hazard on each asset. It can be divided into four stages:

a. **identify the assets:** a list of assets, tangible and intangible, is drawn up with each asset allocated to an individual who is responsible for them;

b. **analyse the potential consequence of a hazard:** this will be determined by the particular methodology adopted (ie quantitative or qualitative) and will examine the elements unique to each asset;

c. **evaluation of the extent of each impact:** this will be driven by the analysis and will usually score each impact on an ascending scale (e.g. negligible, low, moderate, high and severe); and

d. **ordering the impacts:** this involves organising the impacts into a list to highlight the most serious.

Organisations sometimes use a single method of assessing impact for all assets. This is usually done for simplicity and ease of comparison. Common approaches include interpreting all impact in terms of financial loss. Even assaults on staff can be measured in anticipated days off work as a fraction of their wage. However, intangible assets cannot easily be measured in financial terms. Using one method of assessing impact is, therefore, too simplistic and omits to take into account the unique characteristics of each asset and how it is affected by a hazard.

Risk Assessment

A risk assessment combines the separate threat, vulnerability and impact assessments and produces an aggregate value or score for each risk. This will record the 'inherent risk' which is the untreated risk, before security controls have been applied. After security controls have been applied, the retained risks provide the 'residual risk' assessment. An important point to note with any risk assessment is that it can never be completely accurate. The nature of risk, particularly the unknown factors of threat, is very difficult to calculate with certainty and every risk assessment is only an assessment of perceived risk, not actual risk. It is common for organisations to have separate layers of risk assessment, each drilling down into greater detail.

Strategic Risk Assessment

There will usually be a single risk assessment covering security risks across the whole organisation. Strategic risk assessments will include:

a. **threat groups:** such as protestors, petty criminals, disgruntled members of the public;

b. **vulnerable assets and operations:** such as production processes, valuable assets, staff safety; and

c. **strategic impact:** the overall effect on business operations.

A strategic risk assessment will help the organisation draft a security policy which will define the scope and objectives of its security regime.

<u>Operational Risk Assessments</u>

A number of separate risk assessments will cover each security field, such as physical, personnel, personal and information security. Operational risk assessments will include:

    a. **threat attack methods:** such as intrusion (physical security), corruption (personnel security), blackmail (personal security), hacking (IT security), interception of communications (communication security) or theft of documents (document security);

    b. **vulnerable areas:** an area covered by a particular security control, such as communal office space (physical security), temporary staff (personal security) or remote IT connections (IT security); and

    c. **operational impact:** the impact on an asset or operation within each security field, such as premises (physical security) or IT network (IT security).

Operational risk assessments will help the organisation draft security plans for different fields of security which will define the overall approach to security.

Tactical Risk Assessments

Within each operational risk assessment, there may be a number of separate risk assessments focusing on specific areas. For example, within the physical security risk assessment, there may be an assessment which focuses on entry and exit screening. Tactical risk assessments will include:

a. **threat items and tactics:** specific threat items, such as weapons or recording devices, and tactics such as introducing a virus in an e-mail;

b. **vulnerable points:** specific areas which are vulnerable to attack such as a loading bay or wireless access to the IT network; and

c. **tactical impact:** the specific impact which could reasonably be caused by the threat, such as injury to staff or compromise of sensitive information or business processes.

Tactical risks assessments will help the organisation draft security controls within each security field. These will define specific security measures and procedures and describe how they will operate.

Whilst the risk assessment process will start from the top (strategic risk assessment) and work down (tactical risk assessment), it is often found that the lower levels provide a clearer understanding of strategic risk. The strategic risk assessment may be amended as operational and tactical risk assessments develop the organisation's appreciation of its risks.

1.4
Risk Mitigation

There are four categories of risk mitigation: avoidance, transfer, reduction and retention.

Avoidance

There are three main methods of risk avoidance:

a. **corporate level:** prohibiting the organisation engaging in work which generates risk, such as working in hostile environments overseas, working with controversial industries (e.g. animal testing) or working with industries which are at high risk of attack (e.g. defence or criminal justice);

b. **operational level:** prohibiting working practices which generate risk, such as remote working, contracting services to third parties or employing temporary staff from an agency; and

c. **technological level:** prohibiting the use of technology which generates risk, such as allowing information to be saved on removable media or portable devices.

Transfer

Transfer of risk involves moving responsibility for a particular risk to another party. One method of risk transfer is to contract out a particular business function to another organisation which is responsible for protecting that function and the assets attached to it. For instance, the storage of valuable assets could be contracted to a company which provides warehouse services. The company would be liable to compensate the organisation if any of the assets were damaged or stolen whilst in its care. Another method of risk transfer is to place responsibility for the loss of an asset on a third party but retain control of the asset within the organisation. For instance, taking out insurance against theft or damage would transfer the financial impact of the loss to the insurer.

Reduction

Risk reduction can be divided into two categories of protection:

a. **measures:** these are static and provide protection through their presence (e.g. walls, fences, gates and doors); and

b. **procedures:** these are dynamic and provide protection through their action (e.g. entry searching, patrolling, access control and pre-employment screening).

Retention

Risk retention is where the organisation accepts the risk in its current state without implementing further mitigation controls. There are two categories of risk retention:

   a. **active:** where the organisation consciously decides to accept the risk. This can be a legitimate decision where the cost of further mitigation would exceed the value of the asset; and

   b. **passive:** where the organisation has not consciously accepted the risk, but has done so unintentionally, either because it does not understand the risk fully or refuses to acknowledge it.

No security control is ever effective on its own and each will have its strengths and limitations. Those who criticise a specific security control often say 'what is the point of doing this when all someone needs to do to get around it is that'. Each security control makes up a layer which, when coordinated with other layers, filters out different hazards. No single security control is effective on its own, but by arranging a number of them together, a security regime can filter out many of the risks and what remains represents a much more acceptable level. This concept can be described as a sieve and is shown in Figure 2: The 'Sieve' Concept of Security Controls.

Fig.2: The 'Sieve Concept of Security Controls

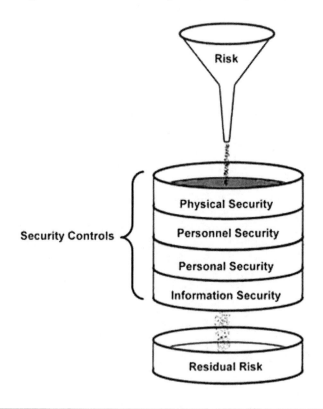

1.5
Risk Assurance

The aim of risk assurance is to monitor and evaluate the mitigation controls to ensure they remain effective. It consists of three stages:

a. **monitoring:** each security control is regularly monitored to ensure it remains effective. In 1.4, it was shown that controls can be either measures or procedures:

- measures are inspected to ensure they are in a good state of repair and are functioning correctly; and
- procedures are audited to ensure they have been followed completely and accurately.

b. **compliance:** appropriate action is taken to rectify non-compliance, including re-training, disciplinary action, increased supervision or changes in security controls; and

c. **reporting:** a formal report is produced regularly to inform the organisation's management of the effectiveness, and any recurring failures, of security controls.

There should be an independent party involved in the assurance process to ensure it is carried out objectively. For example, the security department may complete an assurance report, but it should be scrutinised by the internal audit department to verify its analysis and conclusion. Independent verification also adds a fresh perspective to the assurance process and may notice things that the security department has missed or not considered.

1.6
Risk Review

The aim of risk review is to ensure mitigation remains appropriate to the risks. This involves a re-examination of the previous stages of risk management:

    a. **risk assessment:** to detect any changes in risks;

    b. **risk mitigation:** to ensure security controls remain effective; and

    c. **risk assurance:** to ensure assurance processes remain effective.

The review process does not require all stages to be carried out again. However, a review should consider the approach undertaken, key decisions made and any instances of security incidents and non-compliance with security controls.

There are three methods of reviewing risks which could be carried out across the whole security regime, or a particular aspect of it, including:

    a. **periodically:** carrying out a review at regular timescales (e.g. quarterly or annually);

b. **responsively:** carrying out a review following a change in circumstances such as moving to new accommodation, beginning a new business process or contracting out a particular function; and

c. **reactively:** carrying out a review following a security incident, such as a break-in, loss of information or sabotage to a business process.

Organisations will usually employ all three methods by using an annual review process supported by responsive and reactive reviews as required.

Summary

The concept of risk management may seem complicated because of its many component parts. However, there are four common objectives which can be found in any security regime, irrespective of how basic or developed it may be:

a. understand the risks;

b. mitigate them to an acceptable level;

c. provide assurance that mitigation methods are consistent and effective; and

d. review the process to ensure it is still relevant.

It is important that an organisation understands the components of risk and the relationships between them. Confusion and inconsistency in a risk management process can be encountered if the component parts are not clearly defined. For example, the terms 'risk' and 'threat' are sometimes used interchangeably as if they are the same thing, when the latter is only a single aspect of the former. When planning a new security regime, an organisation should produce a definition of security terms to ensure they are clearly defined and used consistently throughout its security documentation.

Further Reading

Biringer.B, Matalucci.R and O'Connor.S: Security Risk Assessment and Management (2007); John Wiley and Sons

Fischhoff.B and Kadvany.J: Risk: A Very Short Introduction (2011); OUP Oxford

Landoll.D: The Security Risk Assessment Handbook: A Complete Guide for Performing Security Risk Assessments, Second Edition (2011); CRC Press

Merna.T: Corporate Risk Management (2008); John Wiley and Sons

Newsome.B: A Practical Introduction to Security and Risk Management (2013); SAGE Publications Inc

Roper.C.A and Roper.C: Risk Management for Security Professionals (1999); Butterworth-Heinemann Ltd

White.J: Security Risk Assessment: Managing Physical and Operational Security (2014); Butterworth-Heinemann Ltd

Section 2

Security Management

Security management is a continual process to plan, direct, implement and review security controls. This section includes:

2.1 **Security Organisation:** different organisational structures will be examined;

2.2 **Security Forum:** the role of a security forum and the issues it should cover will be described;

2.3 **Security Protocols:** this will describe how objectives, orders and instructions are produced to direct and inform the security regime;

2.4 **Resources:** different techniques will be examined to help provide adequate funding for security;

2.5 **Industry Standards:** a basic process will be provided to help an organisation ensure its security controls are comparable to industry recognised best practice;

2.6 **Legal Compliance:** a basic process will be provided to help an organisation ensure its security protocols are compliant with statutory and regulatory requirements;

2.7   Security Culture: a model for understanding security culture will be provided and the separate elements within it discussed; and

2.8   Security Training: a process will be examined for ensuring staff with security responsibilities are competent and proficient to discharge them effectively.

2.9   Security Equipment: a process will be examined for ensuring security equipment is fit for purpose, is used appropriately and disposed of securely.

2.10 Managing Contractors: the potential vulnerabilities of employing contractors will be discussed and different techniques described for mitigating them.

2.11 Audit and Compliance: methods will be discussed for checking that security controls are applied consistently and taking remedial action where they are not.

2.12 Incident Investigation: a basic process for investigating security incidents will be described.

At the end of this section, the reader will have a basic overview of the main aspects of security management and various techniques and concepts to ensure they are effective.

2.1
Security Organisation

The security organisation is a structure of business units established to manage security roles. There are three models of how security functions can be organised: centralised, de-centralised and outsourced.

Centralised

In a centralised model, all security functions are managed by a security department under its own management. Within the unit there are separate teams which are responsible for specific areas of security. The advantages of a centralised model include:

    a. it is easier to coordinate security across the organisation when it is under a single manager;

    b. dedicated security staff can be employed with appropriate training and experience; and

    c. security staff can focus on their main role without being distracted by other duties.

The disadvantages include:

a. it is often expensive to operate a dedicated security department; and

b. it is easy for security to be seen as an add-on to the organisation rather than an integral part of each business unit's work.

De-Centralised

In a de-centralised model, security functions are allocated to different business units, in addition to their main roles. For example, the Facilities Team may be responsible for physical security, the IT Team responsible for information security and the HR Team responsible for personnel security. There will usually be a security coordinator, such as a senior manager, responsible for overseeing security across the organisation. The advantages of a de-centralised model are:

a. it may be more cost effective than having a dedicated security unit; and

b. it is easier to integrate security into each department's daily work when it is responsible for managing related security functions.

The disadvantages are:

a. security may become neglected if it does not receive adequate priority against each department's main role; and

b. staff may not have adequate security training or experience to carry out security specific roles effectively.

Outsourced

In an outsourced model, security functions are provided by a contractor and only overseen by staff from within the organisation.

The advantages of an outsourced model are:

a. security services can be provided by professional companies so the organisation does not have to spend time building its own skills and experience;

b. security services can be hired when they are needed; and

c. service providers can be changed or contracts re-negotiated when the organisation's security requirements change.

The disadvantages include:

a. the quality of service can be poor as service providers seek to win contracts by providing the cheapest option. For instance, they may pay their staff poor wages which can make them unreliable; and

b. service providers can be inflexible when the organisation's security needs extend beyond the terms of a contract, or may charge disproportionately for additional services.

In practice, many organisations use a combination of these three models when implementing their security regimes, as best suits the assets they are protecting. For example, many organisations have a security department responsible for most aspects of security, but the IT department will be responsible for IT and communications security. A contract guard force may also be employed. When an organisation establishes a security organisation, or reviews its existing one, it should consider which model, or combination of models, best suits its business and ensure all security functions are allocated to a business unit or contractor.

2.2
Security Forum

The organisation should have a forum to discuss security issues and agree on the future priorities of the security regime. It should be chaired by a member of the management board and, as well as the head of security, include senior staff from other business units. The frequency of meetings will depend upon the security requirements of the organisation. In more relaxed security environments, an annual meeting may be adequate. In higher threat environments, quarterly or monthly meetings may be more appropriate.

The aim of a security forum is to review the organisation's risk management programme to ensure it remains effective and proportionate. Its objectives are:

a.   to review assurance reports and consider whether the risk assessments remain accurate and security controls remain appropriate;

b.   to review recent security breaches and incident reports and identify whether lessons can be learned;

c.   to consider the future development of security controls; and

d. to consider the impact of security controls on business operations.

To get the most out of a security forum, it is helpful if there is a standing agenda, including:

a. any changes to the security risk assessments;

b. security breaches and incident reports;

c. assurance reports;

d. new or revised security policies and procedures;

e. forthcoming developments in security controls;

f. feedback from business units on security issues; and

g. notification of any changes in business processes or major events which may have security implications.

Security forum meetings should be recorded on file for future reference. It is also useful to produce a method for recording and tracking the recommendations made by the forum.

Some organisations may have a security management forum with an overview of all areas of security and a number of sub-forums which focus on specific fields in more detail. For example, a personnel security forum could include staff from human resources, welfare, legal and security departments to discuss security risks and controls associated with this particular field.

2.3
Security Protocols

Security protocols are a hierarchy of principles and practices which shape an organisation's security regime. The extent of these protocols will depend upon the size of the organisation and its security requirements. Security protocols can be divided into three layers:

   a. **policy:** a policy is a broad statement of principles and objectives which establish the main focus of the security regime;

   b. **plan:** a plan is a broad description of a particular security process; and

   c. **controls (measures and procedures):** describe individual security controls including procedures (ie dynamic security operations such as patrolling or entry screening) and measures (ie static security features such as walls or gates).

Security protocols can be security specific or be integrated into other areas of the organisation's work. For example, physical security could be included the organisation's facilities management protocols. If separate security protocols are adopted, it is important to ensure they link into other related areas of the organisation's structure.

The diagram in Figure 3: Security Protocols shows three layers of security protocols and examples of different subjects within each. It illustrates that security protocols can be represented in three layers with overall principles at the top which expands into greater detail and focus towards the bottom. This is a useful way of structuring security protocols to ensure individual security controls are linked into a coordinated security regime.

Figure 3: Security Protocols

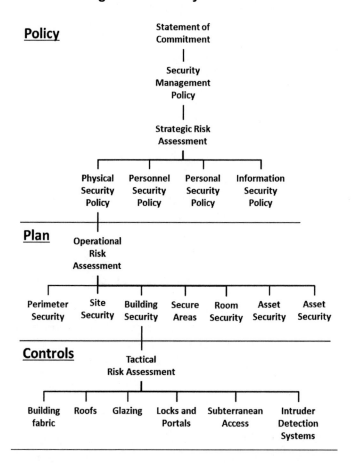

Policy

Statement of Commitment
|
Security Management Policy
|
Strategic Risk Assessment

Physical Security Policy | Personnel Security Policy | Personal Security Policy | Information Security Policy

Plan

Operational Risk Assessment

Perimeter Security | Site Security | Building Security | Secure Areas | Room Security | Asset Security | Asset Security

Controls

Tactical Risk Assessment

Building fabric | Roofs | Glazing | Locks and Portals | Subterranean Access | Intruder Detection Systems

Policy

The purpose of a security policy is to shape security protocols by defining its aim, objectives, principles, management structures, strategic risks and main security fields. It can include the following aspects:

a. **statement of commitment:** this is usually a brief statement by a senior board member which explains why security is important to the organisation and highlights its main principles (eg proportionality, compliance with industry regulation or protecting valuable assets);

b. **security management:** a description of the security management policy, including security organisation, security forum, resources, industry standards, legal compliance, security culture, security training, security equipment, managing contractors, security audit and incident investigation;

c. **strategic risk assessment:** a description of the overall risks to the organisation and the overarching aim of its security policies; and

d. **security policies:** a description of the aim, objectives, scope and background to the main security fields, including physical, personnel, personal, information, IT, communications and document security.

Plan

The purpose of a security plan is to define how specific aspects of the security regime should function. It can include the following aspects:

a. **operational risk assessment:** a description of the risks within a specific security field, such as physical security. It includes attack methods, vulnerable areas and the impact on the specific field of security; and

b. **security plans:** individual security plans describe the overall process within each security area (e.g. perimeter security, site security, building security).

Controls

The purpose of a security control is to describe specific security measures or procedures. It can include the following aspects:

a. **tactical risk assessment:** a description of the risks within a specific security area, such as site security. It includes attack threat items, vulnerable points and the impact on specific areas of security; and

b. **security controls:** a description of the technical specifications of security measures and the operation of security procedures. These are often known as 'Standard Operating Procedures (SOP)'.

The development of security protocols, including policies, plans and procedures, can be divided into the following stages:

a. **formulation:** a single individual can draft security protocols, but it is sometimes useful to use a panel of staff drawn from related business areas. For instance, when formulating physical security protocols, it may be useful to involve facilities management staff.

Legal advisers, auditors and representatives from business units can also make a useful contribution;

b. **documentation:** protocols should be written into a formal document. A template can be used to ensure consistency between different security protocols. Documents should be written in plain English and be concise and clearly presented. Acronyms and technical jargon should be kept to a minimum and explained, either in the text or a glossary;

c. **approval:** protocols should be formally approved by a senior member of staff, preferably by a management board member;

d. **communication:** protocols should be made available to relevant staff, either in the form of a handbook, manual, reference guide or on the organisation's intranet;

e. **implementation:** protocols can be implemented immediately across the whole organisation or in different units across a period of time; and

f. **review:** it is important to review protocols regularly. New protocols should be reviewed after three months, six months and 12 months from the date of implementation. This provides the opportunity to clarify misunderstandings and amend them, where necessary.

2.4
Resources

Security regimes must be adequately resourced to be effective. However, security is often viewed by senior management as an unnecessary cost and is an area where funding may be reduced sooner than other business areas. There are many reasons for this:

a. security incidents can happen infrequently and it is tempting for senior management to accept risks which may never happen when immediate cost savings can be made in reducing security;

b. security is often seen as an obstruction to business practices and keeping funding low is sometimes seen as a method of restricting the negative impact of security;

c. security is often regarded as a back-of-house function and many organisations consider it a good indication of their efficiency if such functions are carried out with minimum expenditure; and

d. security service providers competing for business sometimes make unrealistic claims that they can deliver a high level of service for much lower costs than their competitors. This often leads organisations to pursue the cheapest option rather than investigating the provider's ability to deliver a good service.

There is no easy answer to these views and security must compete with other business areas and accept that it will never be the highest priority. However, there are some measures that can be taken to help maintain adequate funding for security. Not all will be appropriate for every organisation, but they illustrate that security managers sometimes need to think laterally when securing funding and protecting it from budget cuts.

Security Profile

Ensuring security has a high profile within the organisation is the most important measure in keeping it adequately funded. Regular security briefings to staff, security updates for management board meetings and annual security reports are all good methods of maintaining a positive security profile. The quality of security measures is also important. Managers resent paying high costs for poor service. The security department should ensure it maintains high standards of customer service when dealing with other staff, that it responds to requests for assistance promptly and courteously and always seeks to improve its service.

Personal Accountability

Ensuring managers are personally accountable for any security breaches is a good way of keeping security a high priority. This can be achieved by requiring managers to explain a security breach within their remit to their superiors whenever one occurs, or in quarterly performance meetings, or annually in their statement of internal control. This should include a requirement to state what remedial action they have taken to reduce the likelihood or impact of similar breaches in the future. The disadvantage of personal accountability for security breaches is that it can result in knee-jerk reactions to an incident whereby a manager orders the introduction of excessive or inappropriate counter measures because they feel a need to be seen to be doing something about it.

Distributed Budget

Security looks very expensive when it is contained in a single budget and will always be vulnerable to being reduced to achieve savings. However, the apparent cost of security can be less obvious if it is divided into different budgets. Project and programme costs should include funding for security measures required to support them. For example, a new project which requires the recruitment of staff, new IT systems or new accommodation should include funding for the security costs associated with these. Budgets for each business unit could include a contribution to the security of the building. Centralised security budgets should be kept to a minimum and security costs diffused to other budgets to spread the cost of security across the organisation.

Joint Working

Organisations can often work together on security measures and achieve cost savings through economy of scale. For instance, organisations sharing office accommodation could have a joint contract for the provision of guarding services which could be cheaper than pursuing separate contracts. Smaller organisations working with larger partners could particularly benefit from joint working. A large organisation which pays for security services may be able to extend these services to a smaller business partner at a relatively low additional cost. It may cost the smaller partner a disproportionate amount of money to pay for these services itself. Any joint working arrangements must be formally agreed, documented and paid for to provide the organisations involved with control over them and legal recourse if the provisions are not met. Making such arrangements on good faith leaves organisations vulnerable, particularly when the individuals who made them move to another job and their successors may not appreciate the benefits.

Cost Recovery

Some security processes can operate a cost recovery scheme. For instance, a pre-employment screening process will cost administrative time and expense. An applicant may not reveal a criminal conviction on their application form and the organisation could waste money applying for a criminal record check. The organisation may also contract out the screening process to a private company who will still submit an invoice if the application fails because the applicant provided false information. The organisation could require all applicants to pay for their own criminal record check or, if applicable, the whole screening process. If they provide accurate information on their application form, the costs should be reimbursed to them, even if they are not successful in obtaining employment. However, if they have provided false information on their application, resulting in checks being carried out which incurred unnecessary cost, the individual would forfeit their right to a refund and the organisation would recover the cost.

Civil Recovery

The organisation could take civil action against perpetrators of crimes to recover loss or damages incurred. For instance, some shopping centres operate such schemes whereby they will sue shoplifters for the recovery of goods. This is not always as easy as it may first appear and may incur legal costs which are higher than the damages awarded to the organisation. Therefore, although it could enable costs to be recovered for high value losses, it is often impractical for small value losses.

2.5
Industry Standards

The security industry is continually evolving and common standards, best practice and good advice are available which can help organisations develop their security regimes. Reliable sources of guidance can be gained from the British Standards Institute, government departments, statutory bodies, professional security bodies and police forces.

An important point to note is that industry standards are intended to provide guidance to a broad range of organisations with very different priorities and needs. Therefore, they are not immediately transferable, but should be interpreted and applied by each organisation according to its requirements. Industry standards, and advice on implementing them, can be obtained from a variety of sources, including:

a. open-source websites;

b. trade publications such as magazines, journals or books;

c. professional institutes and trade bodies which maintain a library of information or produce newsletters;

d. conferences, presentations, seminars and lectures sponsored by industry bodies;

e. working groups comprising organisations which work closely together, either in the same area or in the same field; and

f. statutory bodies which regulate industry or a particular part of it.

Organisations should continually research standards and best practice across their industry to identify security solutions which have already been developed or where better ways of working have been identified. However, organisations should be prepared to deviate from industry standards and best practice if it is appropriate to do so, provided it does not breach regulations which apply to them.

2.6
Legal Compliance

It is not possible in a publication of this scope to provide a definitive guide to all statutes and regulations relating to security. Laws are continuously introduced and precedents established which define how existing ones are interpreted. Any attempt to list them would become outdated very quickly. This section will focus on the process an organisation should follow to ensure legal compliance, rather than describing individual laws and regulations.

There are many laws and regulations which apply to security and cover areas such as the protection of data, protection of individual's privacy, protection of computer systems and limiting hazards posed by physical security barriers. An organisation must take a proactive approach to ensuring its security measures are compliant with relevant legislation, otherwise it runs the risk of legal liability, criminal and civil, for its actions or omissions.

When considering legal compliance, there are four main steps an organisation should take:

    a.   identify the laws and regulations which apply to the organisation;

b. ensure the organisation's security protocols are compliant;

c. ensure the organisation can demonstrate compliance; and

d. regularly review the organisation's legal compliance.

Identifying Relevant Laws and Regulations

A good security manager, particularly one with relevant professional qualifications, will already have a basic understanding of security related legislation. Industries with specific regulatory security responsibilities (e.g. civil aviation or civil nuclear) will also have a good understanding of the provisions of these regulations. This basic knowledge can be built on by searching the websites of organisations with a role in the security field, including: professional security institutions, government departments, police forces and local government. Organisations may also have close working relationships with stakeholders which have developed good working practices in meeting legal compliance. Rather than starting from scratch, the organisation could consult these stakeholders and consider adopting similar practices. Once relevant legislation has been identified, a full text of the statutes can usually be found online.

Ensuring Protocols are Legally Compliant

Once an organisation has identified the relevant legislation, it should analyse its working practices to determine if they are compliant. The organisation can form a committee or working group comprised of legal representatives and staff with a detailed knowledge of specific working practices to identify security protocols which do not meet legal requirements or are not sufficiently robust to demonstrate legal compliance if challenged. The group could produce a formal report to identify such areas and develop a plan to review working practices and recommend appropriate changes. In some instances, it may be necessary to contract an external law firm with expertise in a particular security field where the organisation's own legal team does not have sufficient experience.

Demonstrating Compliance

It is not enough simply to follow the law; the organisation must be capable of proving it if challenged. Many laws do not prescribe exactly what security controls are required, but simply require an organisation to have a process in place and act reasonably to prevent an undesirable outcome. Compliance can be demonstrated through:

a. **security protocols:** relevant legislation should be described in security polices, plans and procedures with a description of how the organisation will comply;

b. **security training:** staff with security related roles should have legal awareness included in their training programmes;

c. **records:** routine records should be maintained where there is an ongoing requirement to demonstrate legal compliance with a particular process. For example, if a manager requires personal data on their staff (e.g. their entry and exit times from an automated access control system to check their working hours meet the terms of their employment contract), they should be required to submit a data request describing what they require and for what purpose. The form should be kept on file for a period of time to demonstrate that personal data was made available only to authorised persons for legitimate purposes; and

d. **audit reports:** assurance reporting should include legal compliance and highlight any areas where the organisation may have fallen short of its legal responsibilities.

Review of Legal Compliance

The final stage is to seek professional legal advice to review the previous steps and ensure the organisation's identification and interpretation of relevant legislation is accurate. Many organisations have their own legal department, but their experience may be related to corporate law and they may not have experience of working with security related legislation. Therefore, it may be necessary to commission an external legal expert with experience in security related fields to review the organisation's legal assessment.

2.7
Security Culture

A security culture is the shared values and behaviours of staff within an organisation which influences its security regime. It is a very fluid and intangible aspect of security management which makes it challenging for an organisation to control. However, it is also a critical factor in the consistency and effectiveness of a security regime.

Security culture is one aspect of the much broader subject of organisational behaviour. This is the study of how individuals react within groups for the purpose of improving an organisation's efficiency. Whole books have been written on this subject and numerous theories developed on how organisational behaviour can be analysed and influenced. For the purposes required here, we can examine a simple model of security culture which will illustrate the core principles.

Security culture is focused mainly on staff and the factors which impact on their behaviour. It can be divided into three broad stages:

   a. **inputs:** the practical things the organisation can do to influence staff behaviour;

b. **influences:** the factors which can affect staff behaviour; and

c. **outcomes:** the consequences of staff behaviour.

These are shown in Figure 4: Behavioural Factors within a Security Culture.

Fig.4: Behavioural Factors within a Security Culture

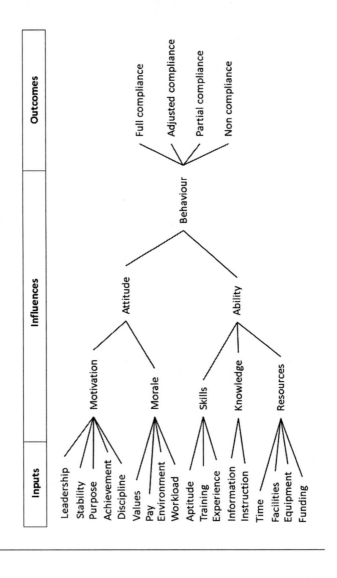

70

Inputs

There are many inputs listed in the previous diagram, which are not an exhaustive list, but provide an overview of the factors an organisation has control of which can affect staff behaviour.

Leadership

Managers must lead by example and ensure they follow the security rules they are responsible for upholding. Managers who breach security protocols should accept responsibility for them and be held accountable in the same way as staff. Senior managers can demonstrate their commitment to security by writing a foreword for staff security handbooks, by ensuring security is mentioned periodically in staff newsletters or circulars and by being proactive in challenging staff who breach security protocols.

Stability

Change is inevitable in most organisations which need to adapt and evolve to suit their business environment. However, change can create instability, uncertainty and impact on morale, especially when redundancies are expected. This can erode the effectiveness and consistency of a security regime. Organisations must recognise the importance of stability in the security culture and ensure changes occur only when necessary and normality is returned as soon as possible.

Purpose

Staff are more inclined to disregard security protocols if they cannot understand the purpose of them. The purpose of individual security protocols should be clearly defined and included in induction training and staff security handbooks. Each individual and business unit must have security responsibilities which are clearly defined and related to their overall business objectives.

Achievement

Giving staff a sense of achievement when they carry out security protocols consistently, is a good way of motivating them. This can include providing bonuses to staff who have demonstrated good security behaviour and including security compliance in annual staff appraisal reports. It can also be useful to generate competition between business units, for example, by circulating a list of units and the number of security breaches each has incurred over the previous month.

Discipline

A reasonable and proportionate disciplinary code is required to enforce security protocols and address serious or repeated instances of non-compliance. This is not always popular with managers who sometimes prefer a less confrontational relationship with staff. However, some staff will only perform security protocols if they absolutely have to and it is better to engage disciplinary measures early on rather than wait until they have caused a major breach of security.

Values

Values are the principles and concepts which staff identify with and support. The organisation should provide documented professional standards to its staff which include a requirement to follow security protocols. Some organisations have a statement of values or a corporate vision which provides high-level aspirations the organisation will strive for. It is useful to include security in such statements.

Pay

Pay is always a significant motivator to staff and their conduct is often directly proportional to their salary and benefits. A good example is security officers who are only paid the minimum wage and are compelled to work overtime to increase their salary. The combination of long working hours, boredom-induced fatigue and low wages will impact on their attitude and behaviour.

Environment

Staff morale is affected by the comfort, safety and security of their working environment. The high costs of office space and the economies that can be made with open-planned offices sometimes result in staff being crammed into large offices. Staff canteens, rest areas, meeting rooms and other such facilities are sometimes considered as a dispensable luxury which could be cut to save money. Such economies, which appear successful in the short term, may have a long-term effect of eroding staff morale, impeding their ability to work to a high standard and increase stress and anxiety. Organisations should consider the working environment they provide staff and ensure it is safe and comfortable.

Workload

Managing staff workload is an important aspect in the maintenance of morale. Staff can become frustrated and anxious by an overwhelming workload which can erode their commitment to perform security protocols effectively and consistently. Workloads must be allocated and regularly reviewed so that they are reasonable and achievable within the required timescale. Where this is not possible and the workload increases as a result of business factors, such a client demands, the organisation must recognise the vulnerability this places on its security culture and consider what it can do to limit the effect as much as possible.

Aptitude

Some security roles require personal qualities and attributes which are not found in all staff for example, attention to complex technical details. It is important than organisations identify the aptitudes required to perform security roles and ensure the recruitment and selection process screens applicants for them.

Training

Security training will be covered in greater depth in Section 2.8. It is mentioned in the previous diagram under the strand of influences relating to ability, but it can also relate to the attitude of staff. Staff who struggle to complete a security protocol will often either look for easier ways of performing it or may disregard it completely. Training ensures staff are competent to carry out security processes and the easier they find it, the more likely they are to comply.

Experience

Experience is an important part of enhancing staff skills and is often accumulated over time. However, some experiences are only seldom encountered. For example, security incidents may only happen infrequently and staff may not have opportunities to detect and respond to them often enough to build their experience. In such instances, it is useful for the organisation to hold regular tests or exercises to provide staff with an opportunity to build experience through practice. It may not be practical to replicate all incidents to the same extent, but it can help build confidence and familiarity of staff.

Information

Staff with a security related role must be provided with accurate and up-to-date information to fulfil their responsibilities effectively. The organisation must proactively research information on the most recent and relevant techniques employed by threat groups and communicate this information to its staff.

Instruction

Security procedures can break down as a result of confusion, uncertainty or misunderstandings amongst staff. Clear, concise and timely instructions are important in ensuring staff know who is responsible for a particular security function and how they should complete it. A simple example is staff leaving sensitive documents unlocked overnight because they were not aware they were the last person to leave the office and assumed a colleague was still working. A rota can be established of staff responsible for locking up the office each night of the week. Instructions can come in a variety of forms including, verbal, standard operating procedures, handbooks, manuals, signs, posters and electronic alerts in IT systems.

Time

It is a common excuse when staff fail to carry out security procedures that they did not have enough time. It is worthwhile for the organisation to calculate the average time it takes to complete a particular security function as it is often not as time consuming as staff may claim. Not only does this provide a useful counter-argument, but it also enables adequate time to be made available to staff to complete security procedures when they are tasked with an assignment.

Facilities

Staff with security related roles must be provided with adequate facilities. A common example is where a visitor has gained access to the building without being signed in or escorted because they were able to bypass the reception or security desk whilst staff were distracted with other visitors. A better reception layout with doors which can only be operated by staff, or visitors with a valid pass, is an easy way to prevent this. Facilities should be designed to support staff who carry out security related roles.

Equipment

Staff within a security related role must be provided with the right equipment to enable them to do their job effectively. The selection and use of security equipment is discussed in greater detail in Section 2.9. The suitability of security-related items should be considered before they are purchased. An example is staff pass holders. Staff have different preferences when it comes to how they wear their pass and some staff may be reluctant to wear it if they find it uncomfortable or inconvenient. For example, maintenance staff may not wear their pass if they are concerned the lanyard may get caught in equipment. Providing them with a clip to attach their pass to their clothing is a better alternative. Such consideration before purchasing items can make it easier and more convenient for staff to follow simple security procedures.

Funding

Resourcing of security has been covered in Section 2.4, but it is worth mentioning here the importance of adequate funding to enable staff to carry out their security responsibilities.

Influences

The influences aspect is the 'no-man's-land' of security culture where the inputs of the organisation conflicts with opposing factors which can divert or impede them. The objective is to influence the behaviour of staff. This is comprised of two factors: attitude and ability. Attitude is comprised of staff motivation (ie their willingness to fulfil security protocols) and morale (ie how contented and fulfilled they are in their work). Ability is comprised of the skills staff have which enable them to fulfil their role, the knowledge they have which informs their decision making and the resources available to them. There are also a number of opposing factors (not included in the illustration in Fig.4) which can counter these influences.

Threat Fatigue

Operating for long periods at high levels of alert, or with very restrictive security controls, can have a deteriorating effect on staff performance. This can be addressed by ensuring that security controls are reasonable, proportionate and sustainable over time. Periods of heightened alert should be kept to the minimum and not allowed to continue indefinitely.

Alternative Training and Experience

Staff may have received security training or experience from other organisations they have worked for which they may regard as more credible. This is particularly the case with staff who served in the military and have been subject to an intense training programme. This can be countered, to some extent, through recruitment and selection which can help identify if applicants are adaptable to new working methods. A training programme can also help align existing skills and experience with the organisation's own standard security protocols.

Dynamic Operating Environment

Staff who work in busy and pressured working environments can find it difficult to adhere to security controls. They may have a number of priorities to balance and accept that it is not always possible to achieve them all. A security control designed to protect against a theoretical threat, which may never happen, is easy to justify abandoning in such circumstances. This can be countered by managing workloads carefully to ensure staff have adequate time to complete security functions. Shifts can be reduced or divided into operational time and administrative time to provide periods when staff can complete security procedures. Where this is not possible and security functions need to be applied during operational work, standard operating procedures should be carefully considered to ensure security controls are limited to those which are absolutely necessary and made as practical as possible.

Peer Pressure

This is one of the most significant influences affecting staff behaviour. Peer pressure establishes principles and boundaries of behaviour which are accepted by a group which may either support or erode the organisation's security culture. In some instances, staff may be fully committed to security procedures and not tolerate colleagues who deviate from them. Security compliance becomes self-administering which enhances the security culture. However, peer pressure can also have a very negative effect on a security regime. A common example of negative peer pressure is the principle that you 'don't tell on your friends'. This can prevent staff alerting managers when they detect corruption or observe security rules being broken. Another common attitude encountered when staff do not follow security procedures is 'no one else does it'. When rules are frequently disregarded and no corrective measures are undertaken by managers, it becomes normal practice not to follow them. Supervision, discipline and regular audit of security procedures are important measures in countering negative peer pressure.

Tribalism

Organisations are usually divided into business units with separate departments, sections and teams. In some instances, a tribal attitude can develop where some units regard themselves as separate and distinct from others and conflict, unhealthy competition and a lack of communication can develop. This can result in security procedures being ignored because a business unit is in conflict with the security team. The organisation must promote a culture of teamwork. Where divisions begin to emerge between units, the organisation must take practical steps in bringing them closer together. This can include providing staff with the opportunity to work in another business unit for a short period of time to gain a better understanding of their work or organising 'away days' or other business/social events to help staff get to know each other better.

Outcomes

There are four main outcomes in a security culture.

Full Compliance

This is the most desirable and involves security protocols being followed effectively and consistently across the organisation. It is rarely achieved completely due to conflicting influences and few organisations achieve it completely.

Adjusted Compliance

This is where the principles and objectives of security protocols are achieved, but by different methods to those specified in the organisation's security protocols. This can occur when staff performing security related roles develop skills and experience which identify easier ways of fulfilling them. This may be acceptable to the organisation and some of its security protocols may be flexible and outcomes focused. However, it is not always suitable for unauthorised, and often unknown variations, to be made to protocols, even if it delivers the required results.

Partial Compliance

This is where security protocols are followed in some cases but are inconsistent and incomplete. It often occurs when staff attempt to make their work easier by following the path of least resistance. They look for short-cuts through protocols, ignore the ones which are particularly onerous or difficult to enforce and push boundaries of acceptable behaviour where they can.

Non-Compliance

This is where security protocols are rarely followed effectively or consistently across the organisation. The organisation may have extensive security protocols in theory, but they are not implemented in practice and have little effect. The extent of non-compliance is often not clearly understood by management and there is a risk that they consider the security regime is more effective than it is.

Managing a security culture is a great challenge for an organisation and is often subject to factors beyond its control. However, it is vital to the success of the security regime and requires continual attention to promote positive inputs and address some of the negative influences.

2.8
Security Training

The purpose of security training is to ensure staff have the knowledge and skills required to fulfil their responsibilities. Every security regime is only as good as the people working within it, but training is often a neglected area, commonly reduced during budget cuts. It is interesting that some organisations will spend a large amount of money purchasing security equipment but spend very little on training staff how to operate it. The huge potential of the equipment will not be realised because staff are unaware of its strengths, limitations and how to get the best from it.

The phrase 'on-the-job-training' is also a common term which could be translated to 'picking-things-up-as-you-go-along'. It often results in misunderstandings, misinterpretations and gaps in core skills and knowledge. That is not to say that hands-on experience is not important during training. However, a clearly defined training plan, including both formal instruction and practical experience, is vital in ensuring that staff have the ability to perform their role to an acceptable standard.

Training can be provided for a variety of needs, including:

a. **equipment:** teaching staff how to use particular items of security equipment (e.g. personal radios, x-ray machines, CCTV systems);

b. **processes:** teaching staff to perform a particular process (e.g. fire evacuation, intruder alarm response, entry screening); and

c. **concepts:** teaching staff principles such as legal requirements, data protection principles, use of force, organisational policies, threats and vulnerabilities.

There are several different levels of training, including:

a. **induction training:** provided to all new entrants to familiarise them with the organisation and the common rules and procedures. This should include an overview of security procedures;

b. **basic training:** provided to all security staff, often broken down into specific security fields (e.g. physical, personnel, information or operational security);

c. **assignment training:** training for specific security roles (e.g. manned guarding, IT network security administrator, vetting officer);

d. **continuation training:** provided after security staff have gained the basic proficiency required to perform their role. It is used, together with experience, to enhance their capabilities;

e.   **professional training:** usually provided by external bodies and enables staff to achieve professional qualifications in specific subjects. Some professional training can be mandatory and is required for certain roles; and

f.   **refresher training:** security staff often learn a broad range of skills they rarely use and periodic refresher training ensures their skills are maintained. It also provides an opportunity to update aspects of their skills which have developed since their original training.

There are numerous models available for developing a training plan and they all have merits and limitations. The following description provides a general overview of what a training plan should include.

Summary of Requirements

This provides a brief statement of the training requirements, including:

a.   **aim:** a short sentence describing what the security training programme is intended to achieve;

b.   **objectives:** a small number of short sentences describing the basic objectives of the security training programme;

c.   **scope:** a brief summary of what the security training programme includes and what it excludes. For example, it may not include IT security which may be included as part of a broader IT training programme; and

    d. background: a brief summary of how the training need has arisen. For example, a review of existing training, a new business operation or a new office location.

Training Needs Analysis (TNA)

This is an assessment of what skills are required by different individuals and how these skills will be provided, including:

    a. training groups: this will identify different groups of staff who require training and can be divided into three levels;

- organisation: the basic security awareness everyone in the organisation requires;
- occupational groups: the skills staff in different business units or who carry out specific roles require; and
- individuals: the skills particular individuals require.

    b. skills analysis: a list of all security skills required by each of the training groups;

    c. training options: an analysis of the training options available, such as presentations, practical demonstrations, role-play or group syndicates;

    d. training method: a description of the training methods selected from the options previously examined, which groups they will apply to and how they will be delivered;

e. **health and safety risk assessment:** most classroom based training (e.g. lectures, presentations, discussions) do not require specific assessments as these are often covered by normal workplace risk assessments. However, any form of practical training will require a health and safety risk assessment; and

f. **evaluation:** how the success of the training will be measured such as by testing, evaluation by the tutor of an individual's performance during the course or simply by the individual's attendance.

Training Resources

This is a description of what resources are available to provide the training and include:

a. **time:** the duration of the training for each training group, broken down by separate modules and measured in hours;

b. **facilities:** the rooms, and other physical locations, required for training and for what duration;

c. **staff:** the individuals, including trainers, guest speakers, facilitators and support staff, required to deliver the training;

d. **logistics:** the supplies and support required, including stationery and other consumable materials, vehicles (if attendees and staff need to be moved to different facilities during the training), equipment and refreshments;

e. **finance:** the money required to run each training course including the overheads, equipment hire, fees for trainers and guest speakers, venue hire, refreshments and consumables; and

f. **material:** the presentations, training aids, booklets and hand-outs.

Training Specification

A training specification describes the requirements of a specific training objective, for instance, entry screening or CCTV monitoring and response. It includes:

a. **objective:** a short sentence describing what this module of the training plan will achieve;

b. **outcome:** a short list of specific skills or knowledge the students will gain;

c. **contents:** a list of each part of the course, including presentations, practical demonstrations and exercises;

d. **timing:** the anticipated start and finish time of each part of the training;

e. **resources:** the staff, logistics, cost and material required to deliver the training; and

f. **assessment:** how the success of the training will be measured.

Review

Experience in delivering training courses will provide valuable feedback from attendees which can be used to improve future courses. Sometimes this can be very subjective and what appeals to one student may not appeal to others. However, feedback from a number of students can help build a picture on what was good or bad about a course. The review process can include:

a. feedback questionnaire completed by attendees at the end of the training;

b. test scores can reveal what aspects of the training students understood well and which they struggled to comprehend;

c. direct observation or participation by a training assessor who can provide a report on the value of the training and provide options for improving it.

Anonymous feedback is often more frank, but limits the opportunity to query a student's comments if it is not clear what they meant.

2.9
Security Equipment

Security equipment is a vital component in an effective security regime. Such equipment can include small handheld tools (such as torches, search mirrors and radios) or complex systems installed over a large site (such as CCTV, intruder alarms, access control systems). If equipment is appropriate to the task, has been set up correctly, is regularly maintained and used by competent staff, it will be an advantage to an organisation. However, it is a common problem that security equipment is purchased hastily after a salesman's presentation, which highlights its many capabilities but does not establish exactly what the organisation needs. To avoid such a problem, the selection and implementation of new security equipment should follow a defined process to ensure it is fit for purpose and used effectively. This process can be divided into seven stages.

Requirements

This stage establishes a broad statement of need, including:

    a. **purpose:** a brief sentence describing the role of the equipment;

b. **objectives:** basic criteria on what the equipment must achieve; and

c. **background:** a brief statement on how the need for the equipment has arisen (e.g. to replace existing equipment, in response to a new or increased risk, to enable a function to be carried out more effectively).

Analysis

This stage examines the factors which will determine the specification of the equipment, including:

a. **users:** a summary of the types of individual who will operate the equipment, including systems administrators, security officers and technical staff;

b. **environment:** a broad description of where the equipment will be used and in what conditions. For instance, whether it needs to be weatherproof, operate in extreme temperature, operate in poor lighting or withstand shock and impact;

c. **budget:** the money available for the equipment, including the quantities required, the servicing and maintenance requirements and upgrades required over its expected service life;

d. **operational constraints:** limitations placed on the equipment, such as restrictions on space;

e. **capabilities:** the minimum performance requirements of the equipment;

f. **standards:** the industry standards and best practice which apply to the equipment;

g. **legal compliance:** the statutory requirements for operating the equipment, or which may apply if the equipment is misused;

h. **timescale:** the time available when the equipment can be installed and ready for use; and

i. **specification:** a list of criteria identified by the analysis with which the equipment must comply.

Procurement

This stage ensures the equipment provides the best value for money and includes:

a. **market analysis:** an examination of the equipment currently available on the market;

b. **tendering:** a process which invites companies to bid for a contract to supply equipment to the organisation;

c. **testing and evaluation:** a process to check the equipment meets the specification;

d. **selection:** the most successful solution is formally approved for purchase; and

e. purchasing: the equipment is ordered from the supplier. This may be formalised in a contract defining the quantity and quality of the equipment required, cost per unit, place of delivery and after-sales service.

Implementation

This stage ensures the equipment is ready for use and includes:

a. health and safety risk assessment: the risks to personal safety through the use, and misuse, of the equipment is identified;

b. training: staff who are expected to use the equipment are instructed on its appropriate use;

c. user documentation: authorised users are provided with operating instructions which describe how they should use the equipment;

d. installation and setup: the equipment is delivered to the organisation, installed and set up in accordance with the organisation's requirements;

e. testing: the equipment is tested to ensure it meets its specification (note: suppliers sometimes introduce new models of equipment which may differ from those originally tested during the procurement stage) and has been set up correctly; and

f. **commissioning:** formal authorisation is required from an appropriate person (e.g. the asset owner or a senior manager) to begin using the equipment.

Operational Use

This stage ensures security equipment continues to be used effectively and appropriately throughout its operational life. It is human nature to look for easier ways of using equipment and this can sometimes lead to short-cuts or inappropriate use. The operational use stage includes:

a. **routine testing:** equipment should be tested at appropriate intervals to ensure it is functioning correctly;

b. **method of operation:** a procedure for using the equipment safely and effectively should be approved;

c. **fault reporting:** faults must be reported as soon as possible and remedial action undertaken;

d. **servicing and maintenance:** servicing includes replacing consumables used by the equipment, cleaning it and recalibrating settings. Maintenances includes checking parts for wear and replacing damaged or expired parts; and

e. **audit:** some types of equipment generate logs of their access and use which can be examined to ensure the equipment is being used by authorised individuals for legitimate purposes.

Upgrades

Equipment is often upgraded or modified throughout its service life either at the request of users or by the supplier. This stage includes:

    a. **proposal:** a recommendation for an upgrade is made describing its purpose, timescale, cost and impact on the equipment's operational use;

    b. **assessment:** a decision is made on whether to proceed with the upgrade;

    c. **implementation:** the upgrade is made and tested to ensure it is working correctly; and

    d. **post implementation review:** the upgrade is reviewed after a period of time to identify any problems which were not identified during implementation.

End of Life Disposal

This stage ensures equipment is disposed of securely and includes:

    a. **authorisation:** formal permission to dispose of the equipment is obtained from an appropriate individual, such as the asset owner or a senior manager;

b. **decommissioning:** the equipment is dismantled and consumable material, or re-usable parts, removed;

c. **sanitisation:** sensitive information is removed from the equipment, such as audit logs or user information and any unique settings or calibration returned to its factory default; and

d. **disposal:** the equipment is removed from the organisation's premises and either scrapped, or sold to another party.

This process is very detailed and, although it may be appropriate for complex systems, an abridged version could be used for simpler types of equipment.

2.10
Managing Contractors

Many organisations rely on contractors to carry out some business functions, such as contract guard forces, technical support, cleaning and facilities management. These parties can include a single consultant working for a limited period of time for a fixed fee, or a large partner company working alongside the organisation from the same premises. The level of influence the organisation has over these two examples is obviously very different and it can impose greater security conditions on the former than it can the latter. Whatever the case may be, the organisation must consider the risks posed by its contractors on its security regime. There are a number of security controls an organisation can agree with its contractors to limit the risk they present to its assets and operations.

Risk Assessment

The first stage in managing contractors is for the organisation to carry out a risk assessment. This should identify what access the contractor requires to fulfil its role, what risks such access may generate and what security controls the organisation considers appropriate to mitigate these risks. Risk assessments can be generic and include a group of contractors (e.g. maintenance engineers) or apply to a specific contractor. Risk assessments should be produced by the organisation, but should also include the contractor to ensure it has an input and understands why certain security controls have been applied. Risk assessments should be retained on record, regularly reviewed and re-assessed in the event of any incident. If the organisation has a number of contractors, and carries out specific risk assessments for each, these need to be compared to enable the aggregate risk to be analysed.

Security Aspects Register

A security aspects register lists the parts of a contract and describes the security risks associated with them. Its purpose is to enable the organisation to record security aspects, and their mitigation, in an easily accessible form. A very simple example is shown in Figure 5: Example of a Security Aspects Register.

Figure 5: Example of a Security Aspects Register

No	Aspect	Risk	Mitigation
21	Access to staff car park for contractors working on site.	Facilitation of unauthorised access.	Contractors will not have their passes enabled to provide access through the vehicle barrier. They must show their pass to the Vehicle Control Post (VCP) which will match their pass and vehicle registration to an authorised access list and grant access. Access will be recorded in the VCP's daily occurrence log.

A security aspect register is particularly useful if an organisation has a large number of contractors and may need to compare security aspects from different contractors quickly and easily. For instance, using the example above, if an organisation experienced a security incident in its staff car park and wanted to know what access different contractors had, it is relatively straightforward to check this aspect across different registers.

Access to Premises

Contractors may require access to the organisation's premises either on a regular and routine basis or at specific times. Such access should be limited to cover only what contractors need to fulfil their role. It is sometimes found that organisations will issue a staff pass to a contractor who only visits once a week, but finds it inconvenient and time consuming to sign in to reception each time. As familiarity with the contractor increases over time, the organisation decides to issue them with a pass which provides full access 24 hours a day, seven days a week. This obviously increases the scope for the contractor to misuse their access for unauthorised purposes. Separate contractor or temporary passes should be produced which are easily distinguishable from staff passes. Their access rights can either be controlled by the Automated Access Control System (AACS) which has been configured to permit access only at designated times. Alternatively, the security officers or receptionists can hold the passes for contractors and issue them on presentation of a photo-ID when they have been booked in to carry out work.

Another issue connected with access is whether contractors should be permitted to invite visitors onto the site. The safest option for the organisation is to prohibit such a practice and require contractors to find a sponsor from the organisation's own staff to authorise a visitor to have access. However, there may be instances where this is impractical or excessively onerous to staff. In such cases, the organisation could permit a contractor to bring visitors on site, but set conditions on how this should be done. For example, appropriate days and times when visitors should be permitted access, what briefing they may require on arrival, how they should be escorted and who is responsible for evacuating them in an emergency.

Work Permits

This is linked to the previous sub-heading, but as it is an important subject, it warrants individual description. A work permit is a formal document, usually produced on a standardised form supplied by the organisation and completed by the contractor, which authorises work to take place. It is used to ensure any access to the organisation's premises, including the removal of assets, are formally approved and recorded for future reference. This helps mitigate the risk of brazen intruders, or contractors with legitimate access, carrying out sabotage or theft and claiming it is part of a legitimate programme of works. A work permit may include the following details:

a.   date and time work is expected to begin and approximate duration;

b.   names of staff who will be undertaking the work;

c.   a brief description of the work;

d.   the location on the site or building where the work will be taking place;

e.   the access required to complete the work (e.g. access to loading bays to bring in equipment or access to plant rooms);

f.   any likely disruption to the running of the site (e.g. turning off utility supplies, excessive noise, restricting access to parts of the building);

g.   health and safety information, such as references to health and safety risk assessments and method statements which can be attached to the permit;

h.   a contact point within the organisation who can answer any additional queries about the work; and

i.   the name and signature of the person who authorised the work.

Copies of completed work permits should be sent to the security control room and/or reception, staff carrying out the work and any other relevant contacts. This makes it easier for security officers to challenge contractors working on the site and verify their claims they are carrying out authorised work.

Access to Information

Contractors will require access to some information about the organisation in order to carry out their work. In some instances, this will be minor details of the operation of the organisation's site such as opening and closing times, delivery times, access control procedures and organisational structure. Such details may be commonly known and not considered sensitive. However, some contractors may have access to details of sensitive business processes, personal data of staff or clients, financial or contract information. The organisation may face serious and long-term consequences if this information is lost, compromised or corrupted by the contractor. There are some main points to consider when determining a contractor's access to information.

Need to Know

This concept (also known as least privilege) requires the contractor only to have access to the information it requires to fulfil its role. For example, a contractor may require limited information from a database. Rather than simply giving it access to the database and letting it extract whatever data it wants, the contractor could be required to submit a data request to the information asset owner for only the data it needs. Another option is to make a copy of the database, remove the unnecessary data fields from the copy and provide it to the contractor. Whatever methods are used to restrict access, the organisation must decide what information the contractor needs and consider the options for limiting such access.

Information Processing Agreement

This is a statement from the organisation which describes how the contractor should process its information. This includes how information should be transmitted, used, stored, audited, destroyed and who should have access to it. The statement should be signed by a senior representative from the contractor to confirm that it is aware of the requirements and agrees to comply with them.

Information Register

The organisation should maintain a register of what information is provided to the contractor, when and in what medium (e.g. hard copy documents, e-mail, removable IT media). This makes post-incident analysis easier. For example, if there is a break-in at the contractor's offices and a number of documents are stolen, the organisation can quickly determine what documents were lost and carry out an impact assessment of the potential damage. Also, if the organisation discovers information has been leaked, it is easier to identify, or at least help narrow down, the contractors who had access to it. The register can also be used to audit the information, ensure it is still in the contractor's possession or that it has been returned to the organisation when no longer required.

Information Custodian

This is an individual nominated by the contractor to be responsible for the information assets it has received from the organisation. They safeguard the assets, provide access to other contractor staff and ensure they process it correctly. Custodians can be allocated according to the type of information medium, for example, a custodian could be appointed to look after all the hard copy documents and a separate custodian to look after electronic documents. These custodians, their name, remit and instructions they have been provided with, should be notified to the organisation and updated whenever changes occur.

Audit and Review

The organisation should regularly review what information a contractor possesses and what information it still requires access to. If a contractor has received a large quantity of information, the organisation could carry out a random check of a percentage of it to ensure it is accounted for and has been processed correctly.

Authorisation to Act as an Agent

Some organisations may require its contractors to act as an agent in interactions with its clients, the public or other stakeholders. This will require the contractor to have authority to make decisions, provide comment and opinions, make statements and commission others to carry out work on the organisation's behalf. This can present the risk of the contractor exceeding its authority, exercising poor judgement, misrepresenting the organisation's position or performing activities which breach regulatory standards for which the organisation retains liability. Therefore, it is important for the organisation to clearly define the scope and limitations of a contractor's right to act as its agent.

Advertising

Contractors will naturally want to advertise that they have contracts with large organisations to demonstrate their credibility within the industry. Many companies have lists of their clients on their websites. However, this can identify the contractor as a potential target for individuals or groups wishing to attack the organisation, but regarding the contractor as an easier target. Such threats may attempt to gain employment with the contractor if they believe it will provide them with access to the organisation's premises or assets. Some threats may pose as prospective clients and question the contractor about its work with the organisation in an attempt to gather information. Therefore, the organisation should consider the risks associated with its contractors' advertising. In some instances, organisations can provide a generic description of its work with the contractor for advertising purposes.

Remote Access to IT Systems

Some IT service providers request remote access to an organisation's IT system to enable diagnostics, user support, or upgrades to be carried out quicker and easier than sending an engineer to site. This poses the vulnerability that the organisation does not know how the remote terminal is secured, who has access to it and what work they are carrying out on its system. The easiest solution is to prohibit remote access for service support. However, this is not always practical as some IT support companies may not have a provision for engineers to visit sites and may only have remote support centres. Also, the costs of sending engineers to site may be excessive and may also cause a delay in installing upgrades to a system. These issues must be considered when IT service contracts are awarded and, if remote access is required, the provider must declare what security controls it has in place to mitigate the risks. Such controls could include:

a. **access control:** a description of the physical, technical and procedural controls it has to prevent unauthorised access to remote access systems;

b. **staff management:** a statement on how many engineers have remote access to the organisation's IT system, what qualifications they have, what personnel security controls they are subject to and how they are supervised;

c. **compliance monitoring:** the service provider should routinely monitor its engineers to assess the quality of their work and identify any suspicious behaviour;

d. **incident reporting:** a formal report of any security incidents which could affect the organisation's IT system. This includes the loss or compromise of any of its data, the loss of a password to the system, any network intrusions, any unauthorised access to the system or any work carried out by its engineers which was found to be improper; and

e. **audit logs:** a log, provided to the organisation periodically, of all access to its IT system, the engineer who had access, the date and time they logged on, the work they carried out and the duration of their access.

Sub-Contracting

Contractors should not be permitted to sub-contract any part of its services to another party without the organisation's prior consent. This can be a particular problem when contractors are under pressure to deliver a service on time and may sub-contract part of the work to another party at short notice to meet the deadline. This obviously exposes the organisation's assets to new risks which it may not have assessed. Contractors should be required to notify the organisation of any requirement to sub-contract work to another company and provide sufficient notice for the organisation to consider the request, and review the risk assessment, before the sub-contract comes into effect.

Intellectual Property Rights

Intellectual Property Rights (IPR) are legally recognised rights to a variety of intangible assets, such as discoveries, inventions and designs. Some forms of intellectual property developed by a contractor for an organisation will be retained by the contractor throughout, and after, their contract. For instance, a company developing an IT system for an organisation will usually retain the IPR for the system, but not usually any of the organisation's data stored on it. If the organisation wanted the IT system to be used solely for its own work, it would not necessarily be able to prevent the company selling it to another party. The organisation should discuss IPR with the contractor before the contract is signed to ensure these issues are identified and any security implications are considered.

Professional Standards

A contractor's conduct may reflect on the organisation it works with and poor behaviour may attract adverse publicity, affect relationships with its stakeholders or incur legal liability. Consider a contract guard force for a corporate headquarters or stewards for a public events company. If their staff behave badly, the organisation's image and reputation may be tarnished and this may affect its future business. A contractor's conduct on contracts not connected to the organisation may also have an impact on the organisation's work. For example, a law firm representing the organisation could be found to have acted corruptly or unethically with another client. If the organisation's stakeholders found out, they may be concerned about the integrity of legal discussions they are having with the organisation. Therefore, it is important for the organisation to identify what professional standards, code of ethics or industry values are relevant to a contractor's work. It should then discuss with the contractor how it promotes and upholds these standards.

Business Interests

A contractor will rarely work for just one organisation. It may have diverse business interests beyond the goods or services it provides to the organisation. In most cases, a contractor's other business interests will be of little concern to any of its clients. However, the organisation's work may be of a sensitive nature and the other business interests of its contractors may create a conflict of interest or cause embarrassment to the organisation. A simple example is if a contractor works for one of the organisation's competitors. The organisation may be concerned that its confidential information could be processed by the same contractor staff who also works for the competitor, and could be tempted to pass the information on. In this instance, the contractor could be required to provide different staff to work on the contract and put measures in place to segregate their working space and ensure information from one team is not available to the other. The organisation should consider what other business interests a contractor could have which would be of concern and ask the contractor whether any of its interests fall within this category. If it does, the organisation and contractor should discuss how these issues will be managed.

Compliance Monitoring

Organisations with long-running contracts should check periodically that the contractor is complying with its security obligations. Where contractors work on the organisation's premises, this is obviously much easier and contract staff can be easily supervised and their work verified on a continual basis. However, where contractors work from their own premises using the organisation's information and other assets, compliance monitoring becomes more challenging. Organisations can carry out random, unannounced inspections of contractors' facilities to observe working practices and how its assets are being protected. Such inspections should be documented and the conclusions, and any recommendations, should be shared with the contractor. Inspection activity can include:

a. examining the physical security of premises, including entry points, CCTV coverage and alarm systems;

b.   examining a sample of records, including IT system logs, test records and security incident reports;

c.   interviewing staff on security procedures;

d.   observing processes being carried out; and

e.   examining signage on display, including posters reminding staff to wear their passes and notices that an area is restricted to certain staff.

To assist with compliance monitoring, the contractor should be required to maintain records relating to security procedures, such as access control logs, security incident logs, daily occurrence logs, pre-employment screening records and staff induction and training records.

Statement of Assurance

A statement of assurance is a formal declaration from a contractor that it has fulfilled its security obligations to the organisation it works with. It can be in the form of a standardised document which lists the contractor's responsibilities and provides a declaration for a senior manager to sign to indicate they have been fulfilled. Of course, the senior manager may be over complimentary of their company's compliance with its security obligations. However, a statement of assurance is a good way of ensuring a contractor focuses on security requirements and has less scope for claiming ignorance if security procedures are found to be deficient. A statement of assurance is only effective if it is scrutinised and any anomalies, uncertainties or inaccuracies are challenged with the manager who completed it. If it is treated as a formality and filed without being reviewed, there is a greater chance it will become a statement of how procedures should have been followed, but not necessarily were.

Contract Terms and Conditions

It is important that security controls are included in the terms and conditions of the contract. This ensures that the contractor is clear about what it is required to do and the controls are enforceable through the dispute resolution clauses in the contract and, ultimately, through the civil courts. In some instances, it may be appropriate to describe each security control in the contract. However, this can make it difficult to make changes to the controls without amending the contract. Alternatively, the contract could reference a standard operating procedure, manual or security aspects register held separately. A clause could be provided that security controls can be updated at any time and the contractor will have a period of notice to adopt them into its own procedures. Some contractors will provide their own contracts which may omit their security responsibilities. They may claim that these do not need to be included and they will follow any reasonable security protocol the organisation requires. The organisation should not except such a suggestion and should insist that security clauses are included in the contract.

2.11
Security Audit

Security audit is a proactive process to check that security controls are being followed consistently and to take remedial action if they are not. Many organisations have an internal audit unit to carry out annual reviews of its internal controls, but the security manager should also carry out their own audits throughout the year. A security audit can be divided into four main stages:

Management

The purpose of the management stage of the audit is to ensure the organisation understands what protocols it is auditing, how it will carry out such audits and how it will review whether its audit has been successful.

Protocols

Section 2.3 described how an organisation can produce security protocols to define its security regime. These protocols are vital to the audit process because they define what standards are to be audited. The clearer, more concise and more accessible the protocols are, the easier they are to audit. When protocols are worded in an unclear and ambiguous way, it is much more difficult for an audit programme to identify if they are accurately and consistently applied. The audit will usually start by listing the organisation's security protocols. It may also indicate how important each protocol is. For instance, some protocols (e.g. staff must always wear their security pass) may not result in serious consequences if a single individual breaches them. It may only present a vulnerability if large numbers of staff regularly violate the protocol. A simple identification system may be used to categorise the importance of each security protocol (e.g. Red – high, Amber – moderate and Green – low).

Audit Programme

An audit programme describes the process through which the organisation will audit its security protocols. The security department may carry out its own audits, but it is sometimes useful to bring in another party who may benefit from a fresh perspective. This could be a consultant, someone from the audit department or a member of staff from another business unit within the organisation. Whoever, carries out the audit should be provided with the security protocols, so they are aware of what controls they are required to audit. An audit programme should consider four points:

   a. **scope:** the security protocols which should be audited. Not all security protocols have to be audited. The organisation may choose only to audit protocols which may have serious consequences if they are not followed accurately. It may choose to omit more minor security controls from the scope of its security audit programme;

   b. **frequency:** when security controls should be audited. The organisation should consider how frequently it wishes to audit certain security controls;

c. **method:** how they should be audited. The organisation should consider which methods it will use to audit different security controls. Security measures (e.g. walls, gates and other barriers) can be inspected visually to ensure they are in a good state of repair and that nothing has been installed close to them (e.g. outbuildings, plant machinery or lighting columns) to provide a climbing aid. Processes can be observed to identify if they are completed fully and accurately and the person carrying them out appears confident and competent. Procedures can be audited by examining the records they generate (e.g. pre-employment screening or equipment testing). Security equipment can be tested (e.g. intruder alarms tripped or alarm buttons activated); and

d. **recording:** how the results of an audit should be recorded. A formal minute can be written by the auditor describing their findings and recommendations. Electronic systems, such as databases or mobile device applications, can also be used to record audit results.

Review

The organisations should regularly review its audit programme to consider whether it is effective and generates results which are useful. Such reviews can be carried out annually and adjustments made to the audit programme before it is agreed for the next year. The internal audit department should be involved in such reviews as its knowledge and experience of audit best practice may prove useful.

Monitoring

Monitoring activity describes the process of determining whether practices are compliant with security protocols. It can be divided into three stages.

Analysis

Analysis involves gathering information on security controls and comparing them to protocols to determine if they are compliant. The auditor will select the most suitable method, gather the information, determine whether or not security controls were carried out correctly and record their findings.

Assessment

The auditor should assess the severity of any non-compliance to highlight the more serious issues from more routine, technical breaches. The auditor may also wish to categorise the cause. This may help analyse a number of breaches over a period of time. Categories can include:

a. **managerial:** management staff may have failed to identify and implement effective security controls. For instance, managers may not have established an access control policy to ensure only authorised staff have access to the premises. They may have been aware of the issue but chose to do nothing about it;

b. **procedural:** a security procedure may be inaccurate, incomplete or impractical. For instance, a patrol route may miss out an area that should be checked;

c. **infrastructure:** there is a weakness in installations. For instance, a fire escape staircase on the outside of the building may not have been secured from external access enabling someone to get into the building without passing through a control point;

d. **technical:** equipment or IT systems may not function as expected. An intruder alarm may not have activated when deliberately tripped by the auditor; and

e. **human error:** an individual may not have carried out a responsibility they were assigned. For instance, a security officer may not have checked someone's access credentials before letting them onto the organisation's premises. It is not usually up to the auditor to determine whether this was a simple oversight, negligence or deliberate act. This is normally a role for the individual's manager or their HR department.

Such analysis can help the organisation focus its remedial action on particular areas. For instance, a large volume of non-compliance due to procedural errors may indicate that the organisation should review its security protocols.

Reporting

Audit reports should be circulated to relevant people within the organisation, including management board members, internal audit department and the security department. The security department should be provided with an opportunity to respond to the audit report. A copy of the report should be retained on file. Reports should use a consistent format to enable the results of different audits to be compared and contrasted.

Rectification

Rectification describes the actions taken to address non-compliance of security protocols identified during audits. It includes three stages.

Remedial Action

Remedial action describes the measures taken to address non-compliance. Appropriate action will depend upon the cause of the non-compliance, including:

   a. **managerial:** new policies and procedures can be developed or managers can circulate minutes or newsletters to staff clarifying any misunderstandings or inconsistencies in their instructions;

   b. **procedural:** security protocols can be rewritten, staff briefed on the changes and old versions of the protocol removed from documentation;

c. **infrastructure:** infrastructure can be modified to cover vulnerabilities or temporary measures installed until such modifications can be made;

d. **technical:** changes can be made to the way security equipment is set up and calibrated or to the way it is used. New equipment can also be installed with different capabilities; and

e. **human error:** staff can be retrained, provided with additional coaching, provided with clearer instructions or put through formal disciplinary action. Working practices can be changed to reduce an individual's workload or provide them with additional support.

Remedial action will also depend upon how frequently specific examples of non-compliance have occurred. For instance, if the same individual continues to make the same mistake, retraining may not be the most appropriate remedial action if it has already been tried. Disciplinary action on inefficiency grounds may be more appropriate.

Tracking

Non-compliance identified during an audit should be entered on a log. Details of planned remedial action should be added and updated when it is implemented. This enables managers to supervise remedial action and ensure it is being carried out. Tracking logs should be made available to future auditors so they can reassess compliance to see if remedial action has been successful.

Re-assessment

Security protocols found to be non-compliant should be reassessed after remedial action has been completed. This can be done as part of the next audit or specifically for each area of non-compliance once remedial action has been completed.

2.12
Incident Investigation

Incident investigation is a process to identify the cause and consequences of a security incident to ensure remedial action can be undertaken to reduce the likelihood or impact of it reoccurring. Security incidents can include minor events such as the loss of a building pass, failure to lock away a document at the end of the day or leaving a PC logged on. It can also include more serious events such as assaults on staff, loss of IT equipment or intrusion at an office.

The subject of investigatory management is very broad and analysis of investigative techniques is beyond the scope of this book. However, many organisations will not usually employ advanced investigative skills for most types of incident, unless serious fraud or breach of regulatory controls is involved. Most organisations will follow a much simpler process which can be divided into four stages, as shown in Figure 6: Security Incident Investigation Process.

Fig.6: Security Incident Investigation Process

1. Initial report

- Date and time
- Location
- Description
- People involved
- Impact
- Immediate action

2. Analysis

Potential consequences:
- Criminal offence
- Regulatory breach
- Contractual breach
- Impact on stakeholders
- Substantial loss or disruption

3. Assessment

Requirement for further internal investigation:
- Proportionality
- Likelihood of success
- Resources (cost and time)
- Negative impact (staff morale, press coverage)

4. Investigation

- Plan (authorisation, objectives, scope, methodology)
- Gather evidence (interviews, electronic data, documents, physical evidence)
- Analyse and review evidence
- Report (conclusions and recommendations)

Initial Report

The initial report captures the main details of an incident and is made as soon as practical after it has occurred. Most organisations have a security incident report form, completed by the first security officer to respond to the incident. The form will usually record the following details:

a. **date and time:** when the incident occurred or, if this is not known, when it was first discovered;

b. **location:** the approximate location where the incident occurred, where applicable;

c. **description:** a brief, factual description of the incident;

d. **people involved:** the name, or a description of an individual if they are unknown, of parties involved in the incident or any potential witnesses;

e. **impact:** the immediate consequences of the incident, such as the loss or damage of an asset or injury to staff; and

f. **immediate action:** what action has already been undertaken, such as deactivating a stolen pass or reporting the incident to the police.

Security incident reports should be centrally filed and retained for a defined period (e.g. 12 months). It is also useful to enter the details on a spreadsheet to enable analysis of incidents collected over time so that trends can be identified. Senior managers and risk owners should be informed periodically of security incident reporting.

Analysis

All security incident reports should be reviewed by a manager soon after being filed to determine whether further investigation is required. In most cases, no further action will be required and the manager should indicate on the incident report form that they have reviewed it and reached this conclusion. When considering further investigation, the potential consequences of the incident should be considered.

Criminal Offence

The organisation should consider whether a substantive criminal offence has been committed, either by external perpetrators or by a member of staff from within the organisation. Seeking advice from the police can help make this determination.

Regulatory Breach

The organisation should consider whether a breach of statutory responsibilities has occurred. This can include a breach of health and safety regulations, data protection regulations or industry specific regulations. Whilst this may incur penalties from the regulatory body, hiding the breach may incur far more punitive sanctions if such concealment is detected.

Contractual Breach

The organisation should consider whether a breach of a contractual obligation has occurred. There may be a resolution process described in the contract which defines what further action should be taken.

Impact on Stakeholders

The organisation should consider whether significant impact may be experienced by stakeholders such as suppliers, clients, customers, partners or contractors informing them early on could help them mitigate any negative impact and they may also be able to help the organisation with further investigation.

Substantial Loss or Disruption

The organisation should consider whether there has been a significant impact on the organisation's assets or business operations.

This process will help determine whether further investigation is required and whether another party, such as the police or a regulatory body, should take the lead.

Assessment

If there are grounds for further investigation, a more detailed assessment will be required and will usually include senior managers and representatives from the legal department, internal audit, press office and human resources. They should discuss the practicality and feasibility of an investigation.

Proportionality

The organisation should consider whether an investigation is proportionate to the severity of the incident.

Likelihood of Success

The success criteria should be defined, such as identification of a perpetrator, identification of the cause of an incident or identification of vulnerabilities in security controls. The likelihood of these criteria being achieved will not be easy to determine early on, but some consideration should be given to whether it is more likely than not that an investigation would be successful.

Resources

The resources which may be required, including time, staff and funding, should be considered and a provisional allocation of each should be provided.

Negative Impact

The potential negative impact of an investigation should be considered. This can include staff morale, press coverage, disruption to business operations and the organisation's reputation.

The discussion, and the final decision on whether to proceed with an investigation, should be documented.

Investigation

There are many different models for conducting an investigation, but a simple four stage process is adequate for many organisations.

Plan

A formal investigation plan should be produced and begin with formal authorisation, usually in the form of a letter from a senior manager. The objectives of the investigation, based on the success criteria from the assessment stage, should be clearly described and the scope of the investigation defined. This is particularly important as investigations can identify related issues which can cause it to expand beyond its initial remit and resource allocation. A broad methodology should be developed on how the investigation will proceed. This may change as the investigation progresses and will need to be continually updated.

Gather Evidence

Evidence should be collated on which to base an analysis. This can take the form of physical evidence (e.g. a damaged asset), interviews with individuals involved, electronic data (e.g. CCTV footage, computer logs, access control logs) and documents. Evidence should be protected from unauthorised access and a log produced describing all evidence gathered, and how it was handled. We will assume that this is not a criminal investigation as this will usually be conducted by police or a professional investigation company. However, the analysis and findings of the investigation may come under scrutiny and the methodical handling of evidence is important in defending the integrity of the investigation process.

Analyse and Review Evidence

Once all the relevant evidence has been gathered, it should be analysed to consider its reliability and relevance in establishing five key facts: what happened, when did it happen, where did it happen, how did it happen, who was involved and why did it happen? Analysis should be factual and objective and emotion and personal perceptions should be avoided.

Report

A formal written report should be produced at the end of the investigation which makes relevant conclusions, based on the analysis of the available evidence. Recommendations can be made such as changes to security procedures, further training, better equipment or disciplinary action. Reports should be circulated to relevant parties and an implementation plan produced of any recommendations, once they have been agreed by senior management.

Investigations are commonly carried out by the organisation's own internal staff, such as its security department or internal audit department. However, private investigation companies are sometimes contracted if complex evidence (e.g. covert surveillance, computer forensics, or document analysis) is required or if it is possible that a criminal offence may be uncovered during the investigation.

Summary

Security controls will never maintain themselves. They need constant attention and support to prevent them being eroded over time. Effective security management is vital to the security process and poor management controls will result in an ineffective security regime.

An important aspect of security management is ensuring it is relevant and proportionate. It is a common fault for an organisation to consider that the more management controls it imposes, the more effective its management process will be. Greater does not always mean better and there is a danger that over-engineered management controls will become bureaucratic and cumbersome. A good strategy is to start with a basic level of security management controls which are carefully considered to balance their value against the burden they may impose on those required to fulfil them. The organisation should regularly review these controls and can increase them where it feels this is appropriate. Starting from the least security management controls and working up is easier than starting with the most controls and reducing them when they are found to be unworkable.

When considering a security management regime, an organisation should consider the following points:

a. **commitment:** commitment from senior managers is vital. All too often an organisation's own senior staff undermine its security protocols because they consider them too petty and irrelevant to their important work. Staff notice and adopt this attitude;

b. **clarity:** security protocols need to be clear and easy to understand. They should be written in a concise and easily accessible format;

c. **consistency:** security protocols must be consistently applied to all aspects of the organisation at all times. Tolerating individuals or units disregarding protocols that do not suit them will also undermine the credibility and integrity of security controls;

d. **communication:** an organisation's security management controls should be communicated to all staff and a source of reference made easily; and

e. **continuous improvement:** security management controls should be regularly reviewed, updated and amended as necessary to ensure they remain effective.

Further Reading

Fay.J: Model Security Polices, Plans and Procedures (1999); Butterworth Heinemann

Kane.P: Practical Security Training (1999); Butterworth Heinemann

Lomas.P and Kramer.D: Corporate Internal Investigations: An International Guide (2013); OUP Oxford

Montgomery.R and Majeski.W: Corporate Investigations (2014); Lawyers and Judges Publishing Inc.

Mullins.L: Management and Organisational Behaviour (2013); FT Publishing International

Sennewald.C: Effective Security Management (2011); Butterworth Heinemann

Sennewald.C: Security Consulting (2012); Butterworth Heinemann

Roper.C, Fischer.L and Grau.J: Security Education, Awareness and Training: Seat from Theory to Practice (2005); Butterworth Heinemann

Section 3

Security Controls

A security control is a measure or procedure to reduce the likelihood or impact of an attack being successful. There are seven broad fields of security control: physical security, personnel security, personal security and information security, IT security, communications security and document security. Each sub-section will start with the overall aim and objectives of the security field and will then examine the main threats. The overall concept of the security field will be discussed and individual security controls will be explained, including:

3.1 **Physical Security:** security controls will be examined including perimeter security, site security, building security, secure areas, room security, asset security, access control and response procedures;

3.2 **Personnel Security:** security controls will be examined under three broad stages of employment, including pre-employment, throughout employment and end of employment;

3.3 **Personal Security:** security controls will be examined under broad headings, including main workplace, alternate workplace, external events, home, leisure, business travel and personal travel;

3.4 **Information Security:** the relationship between the fields of IT security, communications security and document security will be described;

3.5 **IT Security:** security controls will be examined within eight layers of an IT network, including identification and authentication, hardware, operating system, application, network, authorisation, data and protective monitoring;

3.6 **Communications Security:** security controls will be examined, including access control, authentication, hardware protection, emission security, cryptographic security, traffic-flow security and mobile communications; and

3.7 **Document Security:** security controls will be examined around the life cycle of a document, including document creation, document owner, identification and marking, unique material, validation, document register, tracking, access and authentication, storage, carriage and transmission, distribution lists, retention, audit and review and destruction.

At the end of this section, the reader will have a basic understanding of the main fields of security, the different models and concepts within each and an overview of various security controls.

3.1
Physical Security

The aim of physical security is to prevent unauthorised physical access or interference to assets.

Its objectives are:

a. **deter:** to dissuade an attacker through high visibility security controls;

b. **detect:** to identify an attack, or attempted attack;

c. **delay:** to impede the progress of an attack; and

d. **respond:** to repel or apprehend an attack.

Examples of specific threats to physical security include:

a. **intrusion:** unauthorised access to an organisation's premises;

b. **theft:** unauthorised removal of assets from an organisation's premises;

c. **damage:** unauthorised damage or destruction to premises or assets;

d. **sabotage:** unauthorised alteration or interruption of assets or business processes; and

e. **denial of physical access:** obstruction of timely access to an organisation's premises or assets.

Intrusion onto an organisation's premises increases the risk of theft, damage, sabotage and assaults on staff. Unknown intruders include a wide variety of individuals and groups, such as:

a. **casual trespassers:** they may not intend any harm but may use the organisation's premises as a shortcut or to seek shelter;

b. **protesters:** attempt to highlight their cause by blocking access to premises or gaining access to obtain information, sabotage processes or occupy premises;

c. **unbalanced individuals:** may not have a discernible motive but can be unpredictable and potentially violent;

d. **burglars or robbers:** force entry to premises with intent to steal or to force staff to hand over assets;

e. **rioters:** vandalise or loot the organisation's premises and may also attack staff; and

f. **terrorists:** carry out attacks on installations or kidnap or attack key staff.

Visitors may also become intruders if they enter areas they do not have permission to access or remain on the organisation's premises after they are required to leave. An example is members of the public to whom the organisation provides a service who refuse the leave when their demands are not satisfied.

Intrusions by staff or contractors include accessing restricted areas they are not entitled to be in, accessing premises out of office hours or facilitating access to unauthorised persons. Staff accessing restricted areas may not necessarily be malicious and may simply want to talk with a friend or see a business process they are interested in. However, staff can inadvertently cause harm if they overhear sensitive information and repeat it in an insecure environment, unaware of the damage it may cause. Other forms of intrusion are less innocent and examples include showing their friends and family around and letting spouses into their manager's office to help them remonstrate over grievances. Intrusions by staff can also be for malicious purposes such as stealing equipment or carrying out fraudulent transactions.

Burglary and robbery have already been mentioned under the previous heading, but theft by staff is also a common problem. The scale can stretch from staff 'borrowing' tools to carry out some work at home over the weekend to the premeditated theft of large quantities of valuable equipment over a long period of time. Not all theft involves removing property from the organisation's premises. Staff may retain a piece of equipment for their own personal use at work (e.g. a laptop) which denies other staff the use of it and forces the organisation to buy another. Theft from an organisation's premises may also not necessarily involve its own assets. Personal items belonging to staff or visitors can also be stolen and the organisation may feel obliged to investigate and compensate individuals for their loss. It can also create suspicion and animosity between staff which can be disruptive.

Damage to property can involve casual vandalism, such as drunken revellers smashing windows or more premeditated attacks, such as arson. Damage does not have to destroy a large part of a building to make it unusable for a period of time. Damage sufficient to create a health and safety hazard may prevent access or use of the building until such a hazard is made safe.

Sabotage is a subtler form of attack and involves the alteration or interruption of an asset. Examples include altering computer software, inputting false or inaccurate data into computer systems, contaminating products and altering the calibration of equipment so it no longer produces goods to the required specification. The nature of sabotage often requires access to an organisation's assets undetected and knowledge of how such assets should normally function. Therefore, it can often be a form of attack more commonly mounted by insiders.

Physical denial of access can be mounted by protesters or extremists. For instance, access to a site can be blockaded by sit-down demonstrations, by material dumped at access points or by gates welded shut or locks glued. The utility supplies to a site can also be damaged to prevent it from operating.

The physical security model centres on a principle known as 'defence-in-depth' (also known as 'concentric defence' or 'layered defence'). This concept is shown in Figure 7: Physical Security Model.

Figure 7: Physical Security Model

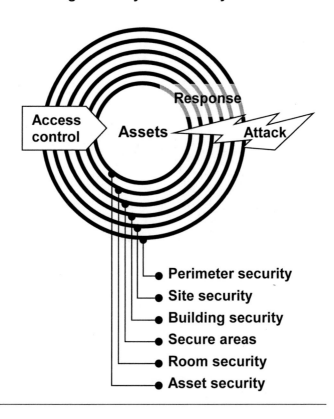

The concept of 'defence-in-depth' relies on concentric rings of security controls around an asset to provide the maximum delay to an attack. A response will aim to neutralise the attack before it reaches the assets. Access control provides a path through the security controls to enable authorised individuals to gain access to the assets.

Defence-in-depth is primarily aimed at presenting as many barriers to an attack as reasonably possible whilst still ensuring that authorised individuals can gain access to assets. However, it also has the advantage that different levels of security can operate between each layer. For instance, fewer and less obstructive security controls could exist on the site, but greater and more substantial controls could be established in areas closer to valuable assets.

Perimeter Security

A perimeter is a cordon around the boundary of a controlled area (e.g. an organisation's premises, or part of its premises). Its purpose is to define the extent of a controlled area, to prevent unauthorised access and to restrict authorised access to designated access control points.

A perimeter can vary in how much of an obstacle it provides. For instance, a rope at ankle height around a lawn with a sign stating 'keep off the grass' at regular intervals may be enough to protect the lawn from damage. A civil nuclear facility will obviously require a much higher level of security around its perimeter to prevent unauthorised access which may have been planned over considerable time and have access to substantial resources. Perimeters need not necessary consist of a vertical barrier. Horizontal barriers can also be effective. An example is wide flower beds densely planted with short, thorny bushes which will deter casual trespass and slow down more determined intruders.

Perimeters can be single-layer (ie one line of barriers) or double layer (ie two lines of barriers running parallel to each other). Double-layer barriers are much more expensive in installation and maintenance costs but have several advantages. They can reduce false alarm rates on PIDS (Perimeter Intruder Detection Systems) if it is installed between the two barriers. Casual trespassers and animals can be kept away from the alarm by the outer barrier, but any intruders which pass through the outer barrier can be detected before they pass through the inner barrier. A double-layer can also help justify a high security response because the outer barrier may require tools (e.g. ladder, sledge hammer or bolt cutters) to get through. The appearance of such a premeditated and, potentially, armed attack can justify disruptive or extensive responses such as contacting the police, deploying a number of security officers or implementing emergency procedures within the controlled area (e.g. locking access to facilities and closing down business processes).

Barrier

The barrier prevents access through the perimeter and can either be anti-personnel (e.g. a wall or fence) or anti-vehicle (e.g. bollards or a high concrete step). There are a number of designs of barriers available and each has advantages and limitations which need to be balanced. It is also important to note the costs of servicing and maintaining the barrier as it will erode over time, particularly in areas affected by inclement weather.

Sill

A sill consists of foundations, or extensions of a barrier below ground level, to support the barrier, make it harder to knock over and prevent an intruder digging under it.

Topping

Topping is used to prevent access over the top of the perimeter barrier. There are a variety of measures for achieving this including barbed wire, razor wire, metal spikes or rotating vanes.

Signage

Signage provides information about the controlled area. It may include warnings of security measures, such as CCTV and guard dogs. It may provide information to legitimate entrants such as the location of the nearest entry point. Signage is also used to discharge legal obligations, for instance to provide information about the operator of CCTV equipment and a contact point to make data requests.

Perimeter Intruder Detection System (PIDS)

PIDS is an alarm system which detects unauthorised access across the perimeter or over a controlled area. Alarm systems usually consist of four parts:

a. **sensors:** to detect intrusion, or attempted intrusion, using a variety of technologies including Passive Infra-Red (PIR), Video Motion Detection (VMD) or microwave;

b. **control unit:** a panel which enables the alarm to be configured, activated and deactivated;

c. **alarm:** a method of alerting others that the system has been triggered. This can be audible (e.g. a siren or bell), visual (e.g. a flashing light) or a transmitted signal (e.g. to an alarm monitoring centre or a security control room);

d. **power source:** a means of supplying power to the system for regular and emergency use, such as mains, batteries or solar panel.

Site Security

Site security is a combination of security controls in outdoor areas between the boundary of main buildings and the perimeter. Its purpose is to prevent unauthorised interference to property kept on site, to prevent unauthorised access to outbuildings and to ensure those on site have a legitimate reason to be there. Site security controls include:

Closed Circuit Television (CCTV)

CCTV provides surveillance of a site and is usually linked to a security control room where the images can be recorded and monitored. CCTV cameras can be fixed or PTZ (Pan-Tilt-Zoom) which enables them to be adjusted from the control room. Cameras can be observed continuously from the control room or recorded for post-incident investigation.

Lighting

Security lighting is used to illuminate a controlled area at night to deter potential threats and enable other security measures, such as patrolling or CCTV surveillance, to function efficiently. Lighting can be continuous or be activated by a sensor or manually controlled by a patrolling security officer or a central control room.

Patrolling

Security patrols can be undertaken by officers on foot or in a vehicle. Guard dogs can also be used to provide a deterrent against intruders. Patrols provide a high level of deterrent and can carry out checks to ensure premises and equipment are secure. They are most effective when they are random so that a potential intruder cannot observe their pattern and time their attack accordingly. The vulnerability with this type of patrol is that, if security officers are free to determine their own patrol route, they may bypass areas they find uncomfortable or inconvenient to search. Some organisations use an electronic tracking system to log when a security officer has reached a specific location to ensure patrols have been carried out correctly. A number of electronic tags are fitted to key positions along a patrol route and the officer reads each tag with a scanner when they reach that position. The scanner logs the date, time and location onto an IT system which supervisors can audit.

Access to Equipment

Equipment stored on site (e.g. vehicles or machinery) should be secured to prevent unauthorised interference. Such measures can include keeping vehicles locked (although this will not be possible on some sites which require keys to be left in vehicles so they can be moved quickly in an emergency), restraining cables fitted to equipment to prevent it being moved, cages fitted around equipment or control panels locked to prevent operation by unauthorised persons.

Building Security

Building security is a combination of controls applied to permanent structures, such as offices, warehouses, outbuildings and residences. Its purpose is to prevent and detect unauthorised access to buildings and to ensure assets and business processes are protected from unauthorised interference.

Building Fabric

The materials used in the structure of the building should withstand physical attack. This can include a simple form of attack by a lone individual with a sledge hammer. With enough perseverance, they could breach a standard brick wall and crawl through. Building fabric can include thicker layers of brick or block, but would typically include other materials such as steel sheet or expanded metal sheet. This is relatively straightforward in a solid construction, but is more challenging in a prefabricated or timber-framed building which has walls made largely from wood or composite material.

Glazing

The windows and frames should be able to withstand physical attack sufficient to deter casual intruders and enable a response to be alerted. Glazing can be fitted with external security features such as grilles, bars and shutters or internal features such as laminate sheets between separate panes. Glass can also be treated to make it tougher. It may be necessary to use blinds or coat glass so that it acts as a one-way mirror to prevent sensitive information or processes being observed from outside the building. This is particularly important where premises adjoin a public area.

Locks and Portals

Any openings in the building, commonly referred to as 'portals', where access can be gained should be kept secure. These include entry points such as doors, shutters and gates, and any other opening big enough for someone to crawl through. These are often overlooked and can include ventilation ducts, utility supply ducts and drainage. The locks fitted to them should also be of sufficient quality to withstand attack.

Roofs

Roofs should be protected from unauthorised entry to the building. This can be achieved via skylights, ventilation shafts and access doors. Entry can also be gained through the fabric of the roof itself with a sledge hammer or axe. Roofs which are accessible from adjoining buildings are more vulnerable, but protesters have scaled buildings with climbing equipment. They are able to mount demonstrations which are highly disruptive as police are unable to remove them quickly or easily and often opt to wait them out. All openings should be secured with metal grilles or bars and any doors or hatches should be locked. Any machinery on the roof, such as air conditioning plant, should be kept secure to prevent intruders immobilising it to make the building unusable.

Subterranean Access

This is a commonly overlooked vulnerability and includes underground access to the organisation's premises. In can include basements or plant rooms in shared office accommodation, service tunnels and sewers and disused basements built over when new premises were constructed. Access points over a certain size (e.g. 500mm) should be protected with a grille, bars or a door to prevent unauthorised access. Finding such access points is often a challenge and the organisation may need to contract a surveyor to research building plans and find all the access points.

Intruder Detection System (IDS)

IDS is an alarm system which detects unauthorised access to premises. The main components of an IDS are the same as for PIDS, previously described.

Secure Areas

The aim of a secure area is to provide a greater level of security in a specific location where sensitive assets or processes are located. A secure area can include a single room, a group of co-located rooms or a floor of a building. Its purpose is to restrict access to those with a legitimate business need and to ensure the integrity of security controls that apply only to specific functions or assets.

Area Controller

An area controller is a named individual responsible for the secure area. They oversee the security controls in place, authorise access, account for sensitive assets and reports any security breaches or incidents.

Authorised Access

Access should be limited to individuals with a legitimate business need. A list of such individuals should be maintained, including who they are, why they require access, how frequently and over what period of time. This enables access to be restricted to such individuals and also provides a list of those who may have had access if a security breach occurs and further investigation is required. Access lists should be regularly reviewed and updated.

Personal Identification

Individuals with access to a secure area should be clearly identifiable. They will usually have a security pass which provides them access to the organisation's premises and different designs of pass may be used to indicate which areas an individual is permitted access to. This makes it easier to identify an individual within a secure area who does not have authorisation to be there.

Acoustic Protection

Soundproofing can prevent sensitive discussions within a secure area being overheard by unauthorised persons. This can be provided by modifying the fabric of the walls with material which inhibits sound waves passing through it. An inner room of double-glazed panels can also be built with an air gap between the inner and outer walls to prevent sound transfer. The access points to the secure area will also require soundproofing as brief segments of conversation may be overheard when the door is opened and closed. An airlock arrangement can be used consisting of two doors situated in parallel so that both cannot open at the same time. Staff must enter the area between the doors, ensure the outer door is closed before the inner one is opened. If the doors have sufficient acoustic protection (e.g. double glazing or a padded core), the conversation should not be heard on the outside.

Visual Protection

Staff and visitors outside a secure area may be able to observe sensitive information or processes through glass partitions or glass panels in doors. Blinds or coatings on glass can prevent observation from outside. Entry points also require consideration, as glimpses inside a secure area can be gained when the door is opened and closed. An airlock system can be used or a solid partition fitted opposite the door to block direct view into the room when the door is open.

Escorting

Visitors, maintenance engineers and cleaners should be escorted by an authorised person who is able to supervise them whilst they are in the secure area. Such escorting may be direct, such as staff being with them at all times, or indirect, such as keeping them observed on CCTV whilst they are working in a particular area. Escorts should be informed of the process for evacuating their charges in an emergency and for raising the alarm if they lose sight of them. Sometimes one member of staff escorts a number of visitors and cannot reasonably keep them all in line of sight all of the time. This may be acceptable in some organisations, but others may set a ratio of escorts to visitors to ensure close supervision can be maintained at all times.

Lockdown

Lockdown is a procedure, usually initiated by an alarm or Public Address System (PAS) announcement, to respond to an emergency, such as a fire evacuation or unauthorised access. It can include locking away sensitive assets, logging out of IT systems, closing access points, immobilising equipment and alerting responders. Such procedures should be kept to an absolute minimum to ensure staff evacuating in an emergency do not put their safety at risk. Such procedures are often incorporated into a drill which is practised by those involved to ensure they can carry it out quickly and efficiently, when required.

Room Security

Room security is a combination of security controls applied to a specific room or group of rooms.

Clear Desk

Sensitive assets, such as equipment, tools or documentation, should be locked away at the end of the working day or when staff leave for long periods of time throughout the day.

Room Access

Physical barriers, such as doors or shutters, should be locked when authorised persons have left the room, even for short periods. This enables sensitive assets to be left out on work areas for short periods during the day.

Key Management

A limited number of keys should be produced, which are recorded in a Key Register, and made available only to authorised persons. A key muster should be carried out periodically to ensure all keys are accounted for. Locks should be changed if keys are lost or stolen. Alternatively, room access can be controlled by an Automated Access Controlled System (AACS).

Secure Isolation of Power Supply

The electricity supply to sensitive equipment may be turned off at an isolator switch which is locked at the end of the working day. This prevents machinery or equipment being operated out of working hours by unauthorised persons. Alternatively, a switchboard could be locked after the switches to a particular work area have been turned off.

Asset Security

The aim of asset security is to prevent unauthorised access or interference to physical assets. The objective of asset security is to ensure assets are accounted for and available only to authorised persons for legitimate purposes. It is not practical to assign individual security controls for every asset the organisation owns.

Controls are normally assigned only to particularly valuable or sensitive assets.

Asset Owner

Sensitive assets should be allocated to a designated 'owner' or 'custodian' who is responsible for them. An asset owner authorises access to the asset, accounts for it periodically and reports any security breach or incident relating to the asset.

Authorised Access

Access to assets should be restricted to authorised persons who have a legitimate need to access them and have been briefed and trained on how to use them appropriately. Such authorised persons should be recorded on a list which is updated regularly and made available to appropriate persons to refer to, when required.

Handling Instructions

Protocols should be established to describe how sensitive assets in secure areas should be handled, including their storage, operation, removal and disposal.

Asset Marking

A tag or label, uniquely marked, should be attached to sensitive assets to identify them. This can include a barcode or Quick Reference (QR) tag to enable a large number of assets to be quickly and easily logged using an electronic scanner.

Asset Register

Each sensitive or valuable asset should be listed on a register, including its description, asset marking, owner, value and other relevant information. The register can be used to record all sensitive assets, identify those responsible for them and help detect when they are missing. For an asset register to be effective, a muster of all assets recorded on it must be carried out periodically to ensure all items are accounted for.

Electronic Article Surveillance (EAS)

An electronic system, such as a tag or token, can be fitted to sensitive equipment so an alarm will be triggered if it is removed from a controlled area. Detectors are required at each exit point around the controlled area and an alarm generated in the security control room or on a system controlled by the asset owner. It may provide an immediate alert to enable the individual to be challenged soon after they have left the controlled area or enable the incident to be investigated at a later date and remedial action, such as remote deactivation or recovery of the asset, to be carried out.

Physical Protection

Safes, filing cabinets or restraining devices can be used to prevent the unauthorised removal of assets. However, safes, filing cabinets, or any other form of secure storage are only effective when the asset is not being used and is placed in them for safekeeping until it is required again. This limits the effectiveness of such measures.

Access Control

Access control is a process to ensure only authorised individuals are allowed into controlled areas, subject to defined limitations. It consists of three stages:

a. **identification:** an individual presents credentials sufficient to identify themselves;

b. **verification:** the individual's credentials are checked to confirm they are genuine; and

c. **access rights:** these are a set of rules which establish the circumstances in which an authorised individual is permitted access.

Automated Access Control System (AACS)

In Automated Access Control Systems, this process is managed by an IT system linked to readers on each access control point which operate a barrier to provide access. In manual systems, an authorised person, such as a security officer or receptionist, carries out this process. For the purpose of this section, the process for administering access via an AACS will be focused on.

Identification can be carried out by three methods:

a. **something owned:** this involves something held by an authorised individual, such as a key, ID card or token;

b. **something known:** this involves a code known to authorised individuals, such as a PIN or code word; and

c. **a physical or behavioural characteristic:** this involves examining a feature unique to an authorised individual, such as their face, finger print, eye retina, voice or signature.

Verification establishes whether the individual's credentials are valid. This involves the AACS comparing the credential to a database of authorised persons. Access rights establish whether an individual with valid credentials has authorisation to be provided with the access they are requesting.

Access rights include:

a. **area:** authorised access may be limited to particular areas for different types of staff;

b. **date and time:** authorised access may be limited to certain days or times. For example, staff who work a standard nine to five day, five days a week, may only be permitted access to premises during these times;

c. **supervision:** authorised access to an area may be permitted only if a certain individual is already in the area. For example, access to a storeroom may only be permitted if a stores person is already inside;

d. **escort:** access may be permitted only immediately after a designated individual has accessed the same point who will provide an escort;

e. **passback:** prevents the same pass being handed back to another person who does not have authorised access. Anti-passback access rights only permit the same pass to be used once in one direction (ie entering or leaving a controlled area); and

f. **security level:** establishes a scale of security levels with increasingly restricted access rights. For instance, if there is an emergency in an area, only security officers will be permitted access.

The access control procedure is carried out at defined Control Points (CP) which can allow pedestrian or vehicle access. CPs may be designated for all entrants or may be limited to certain categories, such as staff, visitors or contractors. Individuals seeking to leave a controlled area may also exit via a CP.

Entry and Exit Screening

An important part of access control procedures is entry and exit screening. This is a process to identify items of security concern on individuals, and their vehicles, seeking entry to a controlled area. The purpose of entry screening is to detect prohibited items which the organisation does not wish to be brought onto its premises. Prohibited items can be grouped determined by the threat they pose, including:

a. **cause injury or damage:** weapons (e.g. firearms, knives, blunt instruments, gas projectors or electric stun guns), flammable and explosive substances (e.g. solvents, paint, compressed gas, or acids);

b. **sabotage processes:** electromagnetic interference (e.g. magnets or electronic devices), and radio frequency interference (e.g. mobile phones or electronic devices with WI-FI);

c. **contaminate products:** poisons (e.g. acids or insecticides) and allergenic substances (e.g. nuts);

d. **collect confidential information:** electronic recording devices (e.g. camcorders or tape recorders), mobile phones or cameras; and

e. **breach legal or regulatory controls:** recreational drugs, media produced in breach of copyright and licensed or prohibited weapons held without proper authority.

The purpose of exit screening is to prevent sensitive or valuable items being taken out of a controlled area without appropriate authorisation. Controlled items can be grouped into categories, including:

a. **high value:** assets which have a high monetary value or are difficult and time consuming to replace;

b. **confidentiality:** assets which contain sensitive information or reveal sensitive details of the organisation's work;

c. **third party responsibility:** assets which the organisation is holding on behalf of another party;

d. **potential for misuse:** assets which could be used in the commission of a crime and are not readily available outside the organisation; and

e. **legal responsibility:** assets which the organisation has a statutory or regulatory responsibility to safeguard from unauthorised access.

Few organisations have a statutory right to search individuals or their property when entering their premises. Therefore, consent from the individual to have their person and property searched is normally required as a condition of entry. If consent is denied, entry is also denied. This is relatively straightforward with entry searching, but is more problematic with exit searching and an individual who does not provide consent to be searched on exit cannot be kept on the organisation's premises. They can, however, be denied future access, have their access rights made subject to additional security controls (e.g. restricting the times they can have access and requiring them to be escorted) or, in the case of staff, disciplinary action.

Response Procedures

Response procedures are a process implemented when an attack, or circumstances which suggest an attack may be in progress, is detected. The responders can include key holders, security officers or police. The purpose of response procedures is to accurately identify an attack, or attempted attack, in sufficient time to enable it to be stopped before it reaches an asset.

Response procedures can include the following stages:

a. **initiation:** a set of circumstances (e.g. the activation of an alarm, notification by a security officer or a report from a member of staff) which provides a trigger to activate the procedures;

b. **escalation:** a step-by-step process which verifies the initiation is correct, assesses the nature and severity of the attack and determines the appropriate action;

c. **resolution:** the method for dealing with the attack and its immediate consequences (e.g. make safe damaged facilities or equipment, administer first aid);

d. **stand-down:** a procedure to halt the response at various stages of its implementation; and

e. **debriefing and reporting:** the facts of the incident are obtained, analysed and reported to relevant individuals to ensure further action (e.g. criminal investigation, prosecution, disciplinary action or a review of security protocols) can be undertaken and the effectiveness of response procedures can be assessed.

Further Reading

Arata.M: Perimeter Security (2006); McGraw-Hill Professional

Baker.P and Benny.D: The Complete Guide to Physical Security (2013); Auerbach Publications

Capel.V: Security Systems and Intruder Alarms (1999); Elsevier Ltd

Fennelly.L: Effective Physical Security (2012); Butterworth Heinemann

Garcia.M: Vulnerability Assessment of Physical Protection Systems (2005); Butterworth Heinemann

Honey.G: Intruder Alarms (2007); Elsevier Ltd

Machette.A: CCTV for Security Professionals (2003); Butterworth-Heinemann

Norman.T: Electronic Access Control (2011); Butterworth-Heinemann

Patterson.D: Implementing Physical Protection Systems: A Practical Guide (2013); ASIS International

3.2
Personnel Security

The aim of personnel security is to prevent staff (including employees and contractors) exploiting their position within the organisation for unauthorised purposes.

Its objectives are:

a. to prevent individuals from gaining employment with the organisation who have malicious intent or are susceptible to improper persuasion or coercion;

b. to ensure employees remain reliable throughout their employment; and

c. to ensure working practices limit the opportunity for employees to exploit their access for unauthorised purposes.

Examples of specific threats to personnel security include:

a. **infiltration:** an individual gaining employment with the organisation for malicious purposes;

b. corruption: an employee misusing their position for unauthorised purposes;

c. deviance: an employee failing to follow procedures or exercise due diligence; and

d. manipulation: an employee being tricked, persuaded or coerced into committing unauthorised activities.

Infiltration is the intentional, premeditated attempt to gain employment to carry out an attack. The scale of attacks covers a wide spectrum from casual criminals gaining employment with a company in order to steal its goods or terrorists and extremists attempting to gather information, sabotage processes or target specific individuals. Sometimes these attacks take years to complete and an individual may join an organisation at a low grade and work their way through the ranks, gaining trust and access as they progress. These are the most difficult to detect because the individual can build a reputation which puts them beyond suspicion. Infiltration attempts may also be completed in a relatively short space of time. For instance, some organisations, such as retail outlets, may take on large numbers of temporary staff over busy periods and not screen them to the same level as full-time staff. Although their access may initially be restricted, they may be able to extend their access, especially if they can gain the trust of their managers and colleagues.

Corruption is the most difficult personnel security threat to counter as those who participate in it may have no prior history of criminal activity or dishonesty and become corrupt because the opportunity is available to them. Corruption is often a progressive act and may start off relatively minor but increase over time as the perpetrator becomes more confident. It can also spread to other staff who justify themselves on the grounds that 'everybody does it'. Corruption can be divided into three categories:

    a. **nonfeasance:** where an individual fails to do something they should have done, such as an auditor turning a blind eye to financial irregularities or a manager failing to address disciplinary offences committed by staff;

    b. **misfeasance:** where an individual fails to do something correctly, such as not completing a procedure fully or accurately; and

    c. **malfeasance:** where an individual does something they are not supposed to do, such as theft, fraud or disclosing sensitive information.

Deviance occurs when staff fail to follow security protocols effectively. Examples include staff failing to lock away valuable assets when they leave the office, security officers not patrolling all the areas they are required to and managers not carrying out necessary checks on the work of their staff. It is similar to corruption, but at a much lower level of severity. It can occur as a result of staff not fully understanding security procedures, cutting corners to make their work easier or through ill-discipline. These may not, individually, cause harm but may erode security controls and make them less effective.

Manipulation, sometimes referred to as 'social engineering', is where an individual is coerced into providing access to information, goods or processes, either by individuals outside the organisation or by staff who do not have such access themselves. Manipulation can include an outsider posing as an engineer or IT technician to gain access to premises or information. More elaborate attacks can include individuals developing a personal relationship with staff which they can exploit. Hostile parties may pose as prospective clients offering lucrative contracts to induce the organisation to divulge detailed information on its products or business processes.

Personnel security controls can be divided into three stages of employment, as shown in the diagram in Figure 8: Personnel Security Model. Not all of these controls will be appropriate to every organisation, but illustrate a range of available controls.

Fig.8: Personnel Security Model

Stage	Security Controls
1) Pre-employment	a) Job advertisement b) Selection c) Pre-employment screening
2) Throughout employment	a) Employment contract b) Job description c) Induction d) Education and awareness e) Access and authorisation f) Probation g) Supervision h) Compartmentalisation i) Compulsory leave j) Tenure k) Separation of duties l) Two-person rule m) Random shift rotation n) Integrity testing o) Counselling p) Discipline and conduct q) Reporting lines r) Audit of processes
3) End of employment	a) Period of notice b) Asset recovery c) Termination of access d) Notification to other staff e) Exit process

The purpose of pre-employment controls is to prevent those with malicious intent, or who may be subject to improper influence, from gaining employment with the organisation.

Job Advertisement

Job advertisements can inadvertently include information of use to someone with hostile intent. Some organisations use recruitment agencies to act as a cut-out between them and prospective applicants. Job adverts run by these agencies will often omit any details which identify the organisation. Applicants will only be informed of the organisation's identity at later stages of the recruitment process. Irrespective of whether an organisation recruits directly or uses a recruitment agency, all job adverts should be subject to guidelines on their content and should not include details of their clients, shift patterns, security protocols, contractors, staff details or working practices. Job adverts should be checked and authorised prior to release.

Selection

Recruitment and selection is usually managed by the Human Resources Department and is separate from the security element of the pre-employment process. However, there are important security requirements in this process.

Identity Check

Applicants should present a recognised form of identity (e.g. a passport or photo-ID driving licence) early in the recruitment process and a copy retained by the organisation. As photographs on these documents can be out-of-date and are very small, the applicant may be photographed before their interview and a copy of the photograph attached to their file. This ensures an applicant does not use false ID from a friend or family member. The proof of ID will accompany the applicant's file throughout the application process. For example, if the applicant is required to undergo an aptitude test or medical examination, a copy of their ID will be sent to the facilitators in advance to ensure the right person turns up and a substitute has not taken their place.

Application Form

This provides an opportunity to gather key facts about an individual, such as their identity (name, date of birth and place of birth), their education and experience. Verification of these details through references or production of documentation is important, not only to ensure there are competent to perform the role they are being recruited for, but also to provide an indication of their honesty and integrity.

Interview

A recruitment interview (not to be confused with a security interview) will often question the applicant on examples of their experience connected to key competencies required for the job. It provides the opportunity to expand on information provided on the application form, to clarify any discrepancies in the information they have provided and to check whether the applicant understands their own application. This last point can highlight if someone else has completed an application on their behalf.

Final Selection

The decision to make an offer of employment to the successful applicant will usually be made by a human resources manager or by a manager from the business unit holding the vacancy. This decision should be made in writing and be subject to the successful completion of pre-employment screening. Security staff will not usually be directly involved in the selection process, unless they are recruiting other security staff. However, they should receive the successful applicant's file, including the interview notes, to ensure the answers they provide during the security interview are consistent. The security unit should also receive a copy of the proof of identity to ensure the same individual who was recruited also arrives for their security interview.

Pre-Employment Screening

Pre-employment screening is one of the most important aspects of personnel security as it is the gateway between a prospective applicant becoming an employee. It can be carried out by the organisation's own staff or by a security clearance company. There are advantages to both options. The advantage of in-house screening is that the organisation has full control of the process and easy access to the documentation if a review is required. The advantage of contracted screening is that the staff involved can be objective and will not have further contact with those they are screening. Contract screening staff may have greater experience and have efficient and reliable systems to carry out the process quickly and thoroughly. Screening companies can also be contracted when required rather than the organisation having to fund a personnel security team irrespective of whether they are continuously recruiting new staff. Pre-employment checks may vary according to the position the applicant is recruited for. More sensitive posts will often require more detailed checks.

Identity Check

An individual's identity should be checked during the recruitment and selection process. However, if this has not been carried out, it must be completed at the first stage of the screening process. The organisation should have a list of recognised documents which can be submitted by an applicant to verify their identity. These can include a photo-ID driving licence and passport, but should also include other documents, in case an applicant does not possess either of these. An identity check for applicants who are citizens of the organisation's home country is often relatively straightforward, but it can be difficult to verify the identity of applicants who are foreign nationals. They may not have identification documents which are recognised and their own national identity documents may use different names, or combinations of the same name (e.g. where first and middle names are used inconsistently). An organisation should have a clear policy on identity checks and refuse security clearance where applicants are unable to provide sufficient evidence of their identity.

Employment and Education History

This should also have been completed during the recruitment and selection process, but will need to be carried out at this stage if not already done so.

Character References

These are becoming harder to acquire as many employers have a policy of providing references only to limited factual statements, such as the dates an individual was employed with them, their salary when they left, their position when they left and the reason they left. The reason an individual left employment is usually limited to brief answers such as resignation, dismissal, redundancy or the end of fixed term contract. However, references are still useful in verifying details of employment provided on an application form. Personal references for periods of unemployment can help fill in the gaps between employment references and should be obtained where a gap in employment is significant, such as more than a month.

Criminal Record Check

This identifies whether an individual has committed a criminal offence which may indicate that they have a criminal career which they may extend to their employment (e.g. through theft, fraud or misuse of equipment) or may be susceptible to manipulation (e.g. drug dependency). In the UK, criminal records checks can be obtained from Disclosure Scotland or the Criminal Records Bureau. Such records will normally omit offences considered 'spent' under the Rehabilitation of Offenders Act 1974, unless the applicant is applying for a job which is exempt from the Act. Organisations may maintain a list of criminal offences which prohibit an individual from being employed, or assess each case on the specific circumstances.

Financial Status Check

This identifies if an applicant has significant financial problems which may indicate they are susceptible to bribery or corruption. It can be done either by a credit reference check through a credit reference agency and/or by an examination of their recent bank statements. However, such checks may not show any money an applicant is receiving, or paying, by cash or through goods.

Nationality and Immigration Status

This identifies whether an individual is permitted to work in the UK. An organisation can be prosecuted if it fails to make reasonable enquiries to ensure an applicant is permitted to take up paid employment in the UK.

Public Profile

This identifies whether an applicant has any views, opinions or past conduct which may be associated with the organisation. An example is controversial views expressed on social networking sites, papers they have published on university or research institute websites and interviews they have given to the press. A public profile check will usually consist of a search of the internet, focusing on press reports, social networking sites and any organisation the applicant is, or has previously been, a member of. This can highlight whether they have expressed an opinion or been involved in an activity which could cause embarrassment or adversely affect the reputation and public image of the organisation.

Declaration

A declaration is usually included in all screening processes which is signed by the applicant and states that the information they have provided is complete and correct to the best of their knowledge. If information the applicant has provided is subsequently discovered to be false, they can be dismissed. Of course, this does not prevent them from making a false declaration in the hope it will not be detected. However, it provides an organisation with recourse, through employment law, if the individual has provided false information.

Psychoanalysis

This uses a questionnaire, completed by the applicant, to detect behavioural and psychological traits. It rarely produces precise and definitive evidence, but can highlight issues for discussion during a security interview. Psychoanalysis can be controversial as many methods lack empirical evidence that the traits identified can be linked to a particular vulnerability or behaviour of security concern. However, some organisations still use them.

Drug Testing

This is an increasingly common form of screening to identify whether the applicant has recently consumed controlled substances which may affect their performance. Organisations rarely have their own in-house drug testing capability and many will have a contract with a drug testing company. A nurse from the company will usually take samples (e.g. blood, hair and urine) under supervision to prevent them being substituted. The samples will usually be taken away to a laboratory where they are analysed for illegal or controlled drugs and a report sent to the organisation which will make a decision on whether to grant employment to anyone who tests positive.

Medical Screening

This may be required to ensure an organisation can meet its health and safety responsibilities towards its staff and that they are physically and mentally capable of carrying out their duties. However, it can also have an important role in personnel security as it can help identify factors which could make an individual susceptible to improper influence. Examples include alcohol dependency, mental illness or a long-term illness.

Security Interview

A security interview provides the opportunity to clarify information provided by an applicant and resolve any anomalies or inconsistencies. It also provides an opportunity to double check important information with the applicant. A skilled interviewer can identify answers which are vague, inconsistent or evasive and help identify false or exaggerated claims by the applicant. Security interviews also provide an opportunity to challenge the applicant's views on subjects which may be of interest to the organisation. For instance, an applicant applying to work for an organisation involved in controversial industries may be questioned on their moral beliefs associated with that industry and whether their conscience would challenge their commitment to the organisation. It also provides an opportunity to follow up on any issues identified during psychoanalysis, drug testing or medical screening.

Employment Contract

The employment contract is important in establishing an individual's responsibilities for security and providing redress in the event of any deficiencies to fulfil such responsibilities. Whilst it is possible to change staff employment contracts, it can involve lengthy periods of consultation and trade union involvement which can make it impractical. Therefore, it is better if employment contracts are not highly prescriptive but simply provide a requirement for staff to fulfil security responsibilities described in a separate document, such as a staff handbook. This enables the document to be updated without requiring changes to the employment contract. Employment contracts can also require the fulfilment of more general security objectives, such as: 'Staff must take reasonable care to prevent the loss or damage to the organisation's assets.' Staff who fail to meet the security responsibilities within their employment contract can face disciplinary action on inefficiency or misconduct grounds. This makes the employment contract a powerful instrument in maintaining staff compliance with security protocols.

Job Description

A job description is a written statement of the specific roles and responsibilities of each member of staff. It is valuable to include security responsibilities within a job description because it helps integrate security as part of an employee's regular work rather than an additional function. It also enables an adherence to security procedures to be assessed as part of staff annual performance appraisals. Job descriptions should not be unreasonably long or detailed and it is unlikely to include a full list of security responsibilities. However, staff with specific security responsibilities (e.g. the custodian of a sensitive asset) should have these listed in their job description.

Induction

Induction is a process to introduce new employees to the organisation. It includes providing them with access to facilities and IT systems, issuing them with equipment and providing them with relevant information. Induction is only the initial phase of staff training and education and will be built on as staff progress. Staff can be overwhelmed with information during induction and there is only a limited amount they can take in. Security briefings should be restricted to basic security protocols and supplemented with a reference source (e.g. a security handbook or the location of security procedures on the organisation's intranet) where further information can be obtained.

Education and Training

Staff can unintentionally compromise an organisation's assets by a lack of knowledge or skills in handling them correctly. A security education and training programme should ensure the following areas are covered and refreshed regularly:

a. **risks to the organisation:** the threats and vulnerabilities facing the organisation and the potential impact;

b. **basic security protocols:** the routine security protocols which apply to all staff all the time;

c. **specific security protocols:** any additional security protocols specific to an individual's work;

d. **asset control:** the responsibilities of an individual to protect a particular asset they have control over; and

e. **security incident reporting:** a requirement for all staff to report security incidents they observe.

There are also more generic security awareness communications that the organisation can implement to help maintain focus on security issues, including:

a. **security presentations:** these can be used to remind staff of basic security procedures or to highlight a particular threat and the security controls required to mitigate it;

b. **security awareness material:** such as posters reminding staff to wear their pass and challenge anyone not doing so; and

c. **security newsletters:** these can be used to update staff on threats and revised security protocols, circulate information on recent security issues and provide advice and guidance on easier ways of carrying out security protocols.

Access and Authorisation

This is a process to determine what access staff require to the organisation's assets. It consists of three elements:

a. **access rights:** defines what assets an individual should have access to and what they are permitted to do with them;

b. **preconditions:** what conditions need to be met before an individual is given access to an asset, such as receiving a briefing, attending a training course or accepting terms and conditions; and

c. **authorisation:** agreement from the authority responsible for the asset that the individual can have access to it.

The main principle of access and authorisation is that an individual should only have access to the assets they need to perform their duties. They should not have access to assets based on convenience or personal privilege.

Probation

Probation is a defined period, usually one year, when a new member of staff will be assessed to ensure they are efficient in their work before their employment is confirmed. The probationary period usually consists of greater supervision and more frequent reporting on the staff member concerned. It provides an opportunity to detect deviant attitudes in staff and highlight any issues which have persisted throughout their probationary period. Those responsible for personnel security should be involved in the probation period and have sight of any documents (e.g. reports, disciplinary warnings, training and coaching) which have been completed. They should also be involved in the final decision whether to confirm or terminate an individual's employment with the organisation.

Supervision

Managers should exercise reasonable and proportionate supervision of their staff to ensure they follow procedures and conduct themselves appropriately. Whilst it is not practical for managers to watch their every move, they can apply some basic techniques to provide a level of assurance on the efficiency and conduct of their staff.

Co-Location

Ideally managers should work closely with their staff to gain first-hand experience of their work and behaviour. This enables them to address issues as they arise rather than waiting for them to be raised by a supervisor or audit process.

Oversight of Staff Diaries

Staff can be required to maintain an electronic diary, accessible to their manager, which records their whereabouts. Details such as meetings, periods of leave, or absence and overtime should be recorded so a manager can maintain an overview of where their staff are and what they are doing.

Daily Records

Staff can be required to file records (e.g. letters and minutes) they have produced on a day file, which the manager can check, before they are permanently filed. This provides an opportunity to review the quality of their work and whether all their responsibilities are receiving appropriate attention.

Process Checks

Managers can check a random sample (e.g. 10%) of processes completed by their staff to ensure they were completed correctly. This is only practical where managers have a good understanding of exactly how a process should be completed, not just the required outcome.

Peer Review

Managers can ask another member of staff to review a sample of a colleague's work to check that it has been carried out correctly. This can be useful where a manager does not have a good understanding of a complex process or where they do not have time to check the work of a large number of staff. However, staff are not always comfortable informing on a colleague's mistakes and may be tempted to cover for them. Peer review usually works better when it is undertaken between staff who carry out the same function but do not work directly in contact with each other.

Official Notebook

Some organisations require staff engaged in operational work to complete an official notebook throughout their working day. Security officers, inspectors, auditors and investigators are examples of staff who may be required to maintain a notebook. Managers can review a random sample of notebook entries or examine entries for a particular case staff worked on.

Some of these techniques will not be easy where managers do not work in the same location as their staff. Some workforces are very mobile and are remotely managed. Managers should consider all available options for supervising their staff and determine which are best suited to their organisation's working practices. Whichever methods are used, managers should be clear and open with their staff about how they intend to supervise them. Staff will often respond negatively if supervision techniques are unexpectedly imposed upon them and this may affect their working relationship with their manager.

Compartmentalisation

Compartmentalisation restricts access to sensitive information or processes to a limited group of people or a specific location. An example is a secure room holding sensitive documents which only a small number of people have access to. Compartmentalisation can be physical (e.g. a secure room or floor), procedural (e.g. access to a limited list of named individuals with strict controls over their actions) or technical (e.g. a database with information restricted to users depending on their access rights). The advantages of compartmentalisation are that it reduces the likelihood of malpractice by reducing the potential number of perpetrators. It also makes post incident investigation easier by limiting the scope of the incident to a specific location and a limited group of people. The limitations of compartmentalisation are that it is not always practical in a small organisation and can create divisions and hostilities amongst staff.

Compulsory Leave

Staff involved in malpractice may not take their full leave entitlement as they fear someone covering their work will discover their transgressions. This can be countered by making it compulsory for staff to take their full leave entitlement each year. Some flexibility may be permissible for a limited number of days to be carried over to the next leave year, but this should be kept to a minimum and staff should be encouraged to plan ahead to ensure they can take all their leave. Managers should be sensitive to staff being overly protective of their work when they go on leave.

Tenure

Tenure provides a limited period of time for staff to hold a certain position or fulfil a particular role within the organisation. The member of staff is moved to another post, or another part of the organisation, at the end of their tenure period. They are usually prevented from returning to the same post for a minimum period. Tenure provides two main advantages. It limits the time staff engaged in malpractice can continue until they move on and a successor takes over. This provides the opportunity for the successor to discover the malpractice and raise the alarm. Tenure also prevents over-familiar relationships developing between staff and contractors which may inhibit their objectivity. For instance, staff may continue to use a supplier they have built a personal relationship with rather than considering if another supplier can provide a better service. The limitations of tenure are that corporate knowledge can often be eroded when staff are forced to move on and an organisation may not be large enough to permit staff to be moved to positions they are suited for. Tenure is also challenging when staff have roles which are very technical or require extensive training and qualifications to perform. Some organisations employ specialist or technical staff on fixed term contracts so they can be replaced regularly.

Separation of Duties

This requires two related functions to be carried out by separate staff to limit a single individual's opportunity to carry out malpractice. For example, most organisations will prohibit the same individual who ordered goods or services from authorising payment. This prevents someone from placing an order for their own personal gain and making payment without anyone else being immediately aware of it. Separation of duties is also common in IT systems where administrators, users and auditors will often have different access rights to prevent someone allocating themselves access rights which they abuse and then delete the access logs. The extent of separation may vary according to each specific situation. In some cases, a co-worker may be acceptable, but in others, a member of staff from another unit may be more appropriate. The disadvantage of separation of duties is it often takes longer to complete a task. One individual on their own could complete a task in just a few minutes. However, the same task may have to wait some time before the second member of staff is free to complete a function initiated by the first.

Two-Person Rule

This requires that a minimum of two persons work together on a sensitive task to reduce the likelihood of corruption. One person working on their own may be tempted to abuse their position if they believe they can get away with it, but a second person present would have to agree to such an action and be trusted not to betray their colleague. The drawback of a two-person rule is that it doubles the staff required to perform the same function and, therefore, will not be practical for all tasks. Tasks which are suitable for a two-person rule include: handling cash or valuable property, destroying sensitive documents and accounting for assets. The two-person rule is most effective when those involved do not know each other well and are, therefore, uncertain of each other's attitude towards corruption. Staff who work closely with each other can build a familiarity and evaluate each other's attitude towards committing an act of corruption. It may also be uncomfortable for one party to report a colleague for corruption if they work in a close-knit team which is susceptible to peer pressure.

Random Shift Rotation

This requires staff to be moved to different duties throughout a single shift in a random pattern to prevent them knowing where they will be at any given time. This is normally done to reduce physical or mental fatigue and is a common practice with security officers. However, it can also fulfil a security function by limiting staff ability to plan a malicious activity with an accomplice. For instance, a security officer planning to assist someone to gain access to a loading bay to steal goods when they are posted to guard the entrance will not know when they will be posted there. They will also only have a limited period of time to arrange for an accomplice to arrive at the loading bay when they are posted there. Random shift patterns are only practical with a large group of staff who are all multi-trained. It can also be resource intensive for supervisors to continually re-position staff and ensure all posts are covered. Random shift rotation requires a record to be maintained of where staff are posted throughout their shift so any malpractice can be traced back to the individual. It also requires continual supervision to ensure staff have not swapped their postings.

Integrity Testing

This can be a controversial security control and involves staff being exposed to temptation, in a controlled test, to see whether they succumb. An example is to provide them with unsupervised contact with valuable assets and covertly monitor them to see whether they steal any. Integrity testing is more acceptable in organisations where corruption and malpractice are a particular risk either due to the nature of the work or the value of the assets involved. An advantage of integrity testing is that it is one of the few methods of positively testing for an individual's reliability and can identify staff who are susceptible to corruption or malpractice. It can also reduce the likelihood that staff faced with a genuine opportunity to carry out malpractice will continue if they consider the possibility it may be an integrity test. The limitations of integrity testing are that it can erode trust between an organisation and its staff if they consider their employers are trying to catch them out. Integrity testing requires a clear policy to justify its use, an impartial and unbiased method of selecting staff for testing, strict controls on the application of a test and the pass/fail criteria and stringent supervision of the process. It would be very easy for mismanaged testing to result in claims of victimisation by staff.

Counselling

Counselling is the moral support provided to staff to help them cope with pressures, frustrations and ethical concerns about their work. Staff can sometimes find their work overwhelming, either due to the volume, complexity, conflict, personal hazards or moral concerns. This can make them vulnerable to manipulation or cause them to disregard security controls they consider obstructive or onerous. In extreme cases, staff can engage in malpractice intended to harm the organisation in retaliation for their grievances. Counselling provides an outlet for frustration and a source of advice and guidance to help staff cope with difficult situations. Some basic counselling methods can include:

a. **manager:** a positive, open and mutually respectful relationship between staff and manager is a good start to effective counselling;

b. **mentor:** a more experienced colleague can provide one-on-one mentoring of a staff member. They can provide a broader perspective of particular issues and advice and guidance on their own experiences;

c. **support group:** these allow staff with similar issues to discuss them openly in a group forum. Staff can take comfort from knowing that others have faced similar problems and can share ideas on how to deal with them; and

d. **counsellor:** a dedicated counsellor can be made available to staff to discuss their concerns. Counsellors can work directly for the organisation or be contracted from a company and can specialise in particular fields such as welfare, ethics or legal issues.

Counselling does not always generate a solution to a problem. Some frustrations or concerns of staff are part of their job and cannot be removed entirely. For instance, staff who deal with the public are likely to face verbal or physical abuse on a regular basis. However, being able to discuss their problems can help staff deal with them better.

Discipline and Conduct

An effective and consistent discipline and conduct regime is the cornerstone of good personnel security. Staff will follow security protocols more readily if they are confident they will face disciplinary action for failing to do so. Corruption and deviance can also be limited through early engagement of disciplinary action rather than managers repeatedly having a 'quiet word' with the individual concerned. Discipline and conduct includes a range of measures both corrective and punitive in nature, including:

a. **increased supervision:** closer and more frequent supervision of staff by their manager to ensure they are following security protocols;

b. **increased audit:** more frequent audit of processes carried out by staff to detect anomalies;

c. **increased counselling:** more frequent and proactive counselling of staff to address the root causes of their actions or omissions;

d. **further education and training:** staff can be re-trained in an aspect of their role where they have made a significant mistake or underperformed;

e. **access review:** an individual's access to the organisation's assets can be reviewed and, where appropriate, restricted; and

f. **security breaches:** staff who do not follow security procedures can be issued with a security breach recording the incident and requiring both the staff member and their manager to comment on it. Some organisations award points for different severities of security breach (much like a driving licence) and a certain number of breaches within a specific timeframe will result in stronger disciplinary action.

Reporting Lines

A telephone line can be established to enable staff to report suspected cases of corruption, if they feel unable to do so through their management chain. Large organisations can run their own reporting lines as operators will rarely recognise the voice of staff phoning in. Other organisations may contract this role to an external service provider to maintain confidentiality. There are some important points when considering setting up a reporting line.

Anonymity

Staff will usually be more forthcoming with information if their identity can be withheld. However, there are drawbacks to providing full anonymity. Callers may make false allegations to implicate a colleague they have a personal grievance against. Also, investigators are unable to contact the caller to obtain further information. Partial anonymity can be granted by requiring the caller to provide contact details to the operator but this information is withheld from anyone else in the organisation. If further information or clarification of specific points is required, the investigators can provide these questions to the operator who can contact the caller and relay their answers back to the investigators.

Confidentiality

Information provided to reporting lines must be restricted to a limited number of people tasked with investigating the claims. Even where a caller's identity is protected, widespread knowledge that an investigation has been launched following a call to the reporting line, could spark debate amongst staff about the origin of the call. This may concern the caller that they may be discovered, especially if specific details of their complaint are widely released. Information provided to the reporting line must be kept confidential and only the general points released to staff who are contacted as part of the investigation.

Recording

A simple but important point to consider is how information provided to the reporting line will be recorded. Phone calls can be saved as an audio recording which ensures information is preserved in its original and accurate form. However, the recording must be kept confidential to protect the anonymity of the caller. A typed verbatim record can be made of the call for investigators. A written record of the main facts of the call can also be made by operators, either typed or handwritten, on a template document and passed to the investigators. Whichever method is used, it is important to ensure a complete and accurate record of the call is made to prevent misinterpretations arising when the information is forwarded to investigators and its original meaning is distorted.

Training of Operators

Operators need to keep calm so they can deal with callers who may be angry or frustrated. They should also be trained to capture the relevant information as quickly as possible as callers may only intend to be on the phone for a short period of time and may hang up abruptly. Operators should also be trained to record information accurately. The more factual details they are able to obtain, the more the investigators will have to work on.

Audit of Processes

Working processes should be subject to regular audit to detect anomalies which may indicate corruption or deviance. Larger organisations will usually have dedicated audit units, but smaller ones may rely on managers to carry out this role. It is impractical to audit every action and process, but checking a random sample can provide a deterrent to corruption and help identify such practices if they do occur. For an audit system to be effective, processes must generate an audit trail. This can be in the form of logs, forms, CCTV, or photographs. All processes required to be audited, and particularly those vulnerable to corruption, must be required to generate an audit trail. Such trails are most effective when the evidence is generated and stored by a party other than those involved in the process itself. This prevents audit trails being altered or erased to hide corrupt practices.

Access Review

An access review is a formal process to assess an individual's continued need to have access to sensitive or valuable assets. Such assets can include premises, tools, equipment, IT systems or files. Even where an individual remains in the same post, the nature of their work may change and the access rights with which they were originally provided may no longer be required. Access rights should be reviewed whenever an individual moves posts within the organisation. Staff who remain in the same post should have their access rights reviewed regularly.

An access review can take the form of a document (either hard copy or electronic), prepared by the asset owner and sent to the individual's manager for review. If the manager is satisfied that all access listed within the document is still required by the individual, they approve the list and return it to the asset owner. Alternatively, the manager can advise that access rights be restricted or revoked. Asset owners may also challenge access rights they consider unusual or excessive and ask a manager to provide further justification of why the individual requires such access.

Period of Notice

When an individual resigns, or is made redundant, they are usually provided with a period of notice, typically between 30 days to three months. During this period, they may be disgruntled or less focused on completing their duties diligently. The organisation should consider whether staff should continue their normal work throughout their period of notice, when there may be greater temptation for them to cause disruption or damage. The options available to the organisation include:

a. **business as usual:** permitting the individual to continue working exactly as they have done throughout their period of notice. This is a reasonable option where the individual is still considered to be reliable or may not have access to sensitive or valuable assets;

b. **additional supervision:** the individual continues working as normal, but has additional supervision from their manager during their period of notice;

c. **additional audit:** the individual continues working as normal, but their work is subject to an increase in the scope or frequency of audit checks;

d. **reduced responsibilities and access rights:** the more sensitive responsibilities of the individual are removed during their period of notice and their access rights to information or assets required to complete these responsibilities are also revoked; or

e. **immediate departure:** an individual may not be permitted to work their period of notice and may be required to leave immediately.

Asset Recovery

The assets provided to an individual in the course of their employment must be recovered before they leave. The organisation's asset register will list the assets issued to members of staff which can be forwarded to their manager. The manager can ensure the assets are recovered before they depart and amend the asset register accordingly. Assets not returned by an individual when they leave should be notified to the asset owner, internal audit and the security department. The recovery of assets from staff who have left the organisation can be difficult, especially if the individual feels animosity towards their former employer. The options available to the organisation in such instances includes writing the asset off as a loss, civil litigation or criminal prosecution.

Termination of Access

An individual's access rights to premises, information and IT systems must be revoked when they leave the organisation. This process may begin before their actual leave date. For example, a human resources manager may be prevented from taking on new case work during their period of notice and their access rights to personnel files may be withdrawn. Such staged withdrawal of access rights may be discussed between the individual's manager and the relevant asset owner, but the organisation may provide guidelines on the withdrawal of access rights during periods of notice to ensure a consistent approach.

Individuals who leave the organisation on a temporary basis (e.g. on maternity/paternity leave, long-term sickness, career break or suspension during investigation) may have their access rights suspended but not completed revoked. This will make is quicker and easier for their access rights to be reinstated without them needing to reapply for them. All remaining access rights must be automatically revoked on the individual's last day in the organisation.

Notification of Departure

When an individual leaves an organisation, it is important that colleagues are informed of their departure. This prevents the individual contacting them and pretending to still be employed in order to gain access to information or assets they are no longer entitled to. Immediate colleagues will obviously be aware of their departure, but colleagues in other departments, such as the IT service desk, may not and could unwittingly provide the individual with information or access over the phone. Such notifications can be generic and include a list of all staff who have left the organisation over the previous week. However, notifications of a specific member of staff's departure may be circulated, especially if they worked in a sensitive position. Notices can also be provided to security staff for inclusion in handover briefings or post notes.

Exit Process

The point at which an individual leaves an organisation provides a final opportunity to recover any equipment or documentation they have been issued with. Once they leave, it is much more difficult to follow up any outstanding issues. A formal exit procedure should be established which could include:

a. **exit declaration:** a statement, completed by the individual, stating that all property belonging to the organisation which they were issued with during their employment has been returned and acknowledging any ongoing contractual obligations they may have;

b. **removal of access rights:** a formal check to ensure that all the access rights the individual has been given throughout their employment have been terminated;

c. **exit interview:** a formal discussion with the individual to remind them of their ongoing responsibilities towards the confidentiality of the organisation's information and to cover any issues that concerned them during their employment. Staff may be more forthcoming with information about corruption when they are leaving and are no longer concerned about any repercussions from their former colleagues; and

d. **escort from the premises:** this will depend upon the circumstances and someone retiring may be treated differently to someone who has been dismissed. Escorting from the premises need not be heavy handed and a manager can offer to walk their former staff out and take one last opportunity to thank them for their work.

Further Reading

Appel. E: Cybervetting: Internet Searches for Vetting, Investigations, and Open-Source Intelligence, Second Edition (2014); CRC Press

Blackwell.C: The Insider Threat: Combatting the Enemy Within (2009); ITGP

Colaprete. F: Pre-Employment Background Investigations for Public Safety Professionals (2012); CRC Press

Graycar.A and Prenzier.T: Understanding and Preventing Corruption – Crime Prevention and Security Management (2013); Palgrave Pivot

Nixon.B and Kerr.K: Background Screening and Investigations: Managing Hiring Risk from the HR and Security Perspectives (2008); Butterworth Heinemann

Rideout.H: Employee Risk Management: How to Protect Your Business Reputation and Reduce Your Legal Liability (2014); Kogan Page

Shepherd.E and Griffiths.A: Investigative Interviewing: The Conversation Management Approach (2013); OUP Oxford

3.3
Personal Security

The aim of personal security is to protect an individual, their property, privacy, integrity and reputation from improper interference or influence.

Its objectives are:

a. **person:** to protect an individual's person from harm;

b. **property:** to protect an individual's property from unlawful damage or interference;

c. **privacy:** to protect an individual's privacy from undue intrusion; and

d. **pressure:** to protect an individual's will from undue pressure or manipulation.

Examples of specific threats to personal security include:

a. **assault:** the use of force, or threat of force, against an individual. This can be directly (e.g. by physical attack) or indirectly (e.g. threatening phone calls);

b. **criminal damage:** pressure can be exerted on staff by vandalising their personal property such as their car or their home;

c. **kidnap:** the unlawful detention of an individual to extract a financial or political penalty in exchange for their release;

d. **coercion:** improper influence over an individual to make a decision, or undertake an action, that they would not otherwise make;

e. **compromise:** to damage the integrity or reputation of an individual by associating them with views, opinions or actions which are considered unlawful, unethical or contrary to their public or private status; and

f. **invasion of privacy:** unauthorised access to personal information about an individual that they would wish to keep private.

Assault is one of the most common threats to personal security. It can range from casual violence encountered by reception staff or security officers, to premeditated attacks targeting specific members of staff. It does not have to be physical and threats can be equally effective in impeding staff from carrying out their functions, demotivating them or forcing them to resign.

Criminal damage of staff property can inflict significant psychological pressure on its victim, especially where there is a threat of escalation. However, it can also have a more tangible impact. Staff may need to take time off work to arrange for repairs or the increasing cost may force them to resign to stop the attacks.

Kidnapping is not only a risk to senior and wealthy CEOs, but to more junior staff who can provide access to the organisation's premises or assets. For example, the cleaner or security guard could be kidnapped and forced by a criminal to provide access to a warehouse storing valuable goods. Kidnapping also does not necessary have to be targeted at a specific individual. Random staff can be snatched to put pressure on an organisation to cease an activity opposed by the kidnappers. Of course, wealthy CEOs often have a high public profile, and their home may have been identified in press reports, making them an easier target for kidnappers than other members of staff.

Coercion can involve persuasion, threats or a combination of both to induce a member of staff to behave in a way they would not otherwise choose. Examples of coercion can involve bribery, blackmail, physical and verbal intimidation and pressure from family or social group. It can often take place over a long period of time, and even small levels of coercion can build to intolerable levels on an individual.

Compromise can either be passive, such as watching and waiting for an individual to express a view or engage in an action which could lead to compromise. It can also be more active, such as provoking an individual into such a position. The latter is commonly known as 'entrapment' and can involve tempting an individual to engage in an illegal or immoral activity and recording it. Minor compromises may cause embarrassment or adverse press coverage which passes with time with no persistent ill-effects. However, more serious compromise can result in forced resignations, dismissal or even prosecution.

Invasion of privacy can range from searching litter bins for personal documents which have been thrown away, intercepting mail, unwelcome house calls, trawling the internet for personal profiles on social networking sites or following an individual to build up a picture of their pattern of life. Invasion of privacy can be used by hostile groups to research information which may help them launch another form of attack or as a means of harassing staff.

The concept of personal security is based on an individual's 'pattern of life' which describes their usual movements around their professional and personal lives. This concept is shown in Figure 9: Pattern of Life Model.

Fig.9: Pattern of Life Model

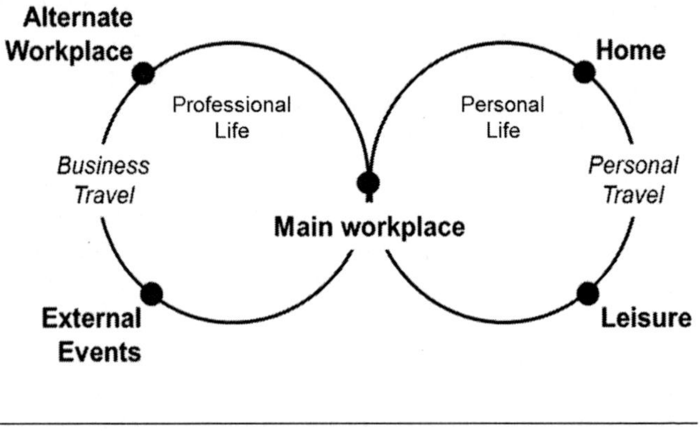

An individual's pattern of life is commonly organised around a figure of eight pattern of professional and personal life, joined by their main workplace and linked by personal and business travel.

Workplace Security

Workplace security is covered, to a large extent, by the normal security controls the organisation has installed on its premises. However, there are some specific areas of the workplace where security controls should focus on the personal security of staff.

Vulnerable Points

A Vulnerable Point (VP) is a specific area in a physical security plan where an attack would be most successful. When considering the personal security of staff, there are a number of areas in the workplace where attacks (physical and verbal) commonly occur.

Receptions are where most visitors to the organisation first engage with staff. It can be a focal point for aggression and conflict. This can range from a contractor who arrives but is not scheduled to work that day, a courier delayed because their delivery is unexpected or other members of staff with a faulty pass which does not work on the access control system. Such individuals can become short tempered which can escalate to intimidating or violent behaviour. An organisation which is engaged in controversial business practices may experience protesters or intruders to its reception area who may assault the reception staff. The physical security of reception areas should be considered, including barriers, access control, CCTV and Personal Alarm Buttons (PAB). The items accessible to visitors in the reception area must also be considered. Plant pots, chairs, fire extinguishers and waste bins can be used as weapons to assault staff. Reception staff should be trained in conflict management, so they have skills to help them respond constructively to aggressive behaviour before it escalates.

The organisation may meet with clients, contractors or other external individuals and the meeting room is a potential flashpoint for abusive or violent behaviour. Where practical, specific meeting rooms close to an entrance can be dedicated to external meetings. Physical security measures such as CCTV and PABs can be installed. Security officers can be stationed outside the room during meetings which may become heated or contentious to act as a deterrent and provide a response, if required. The room layout can be arranged to keep the organisation's staff and external individuals separate to provide a reaction time against a physical attack. Consideration should be given to items which could be used as a weapon (e.g. chairs, plant pots, fire extinguishers). Chairs can be fixed to the floor or a design chosen which is heavy or unwieldy. Fire extinguishers can be kept outside the meeting room and unnecessary items such as plant pots removed.

A loading bay often includes large access points which are left open for periods of time whilst goods are off-loaded. These can attract attention from those attempting to access the building or to steal deliveries. Staff can be assaulted or threatened in such attacks. The best solution is to have an 'airlock' arrangement where a loading area is covered by gates or shutters at either end with enough room between for a lorry to park. One gate or shutter will always be kept closed to protect staff when off-loading. However, this option can be costly and impractical in some circumstances. Alternative security measures include having a security officer present during deliveries, good CCTV coverage of the loading area and having random delivery times for high value goods.

Where organisations have a staff car park adjacent to their premises, they should consider the vulnerability of staff and their cars. Car parks can attract petty thieves and vandals, but can also be a focal point for attackers with a grievance against the organisation. Parking spaces reserved for senior managers may have their position marked (e.g. 'reserved for CEO') which could make the car parked there a target for vandals or anyone getting in or out of the car a target for physical or verbal abuse. Staff returning to their cars in the evening after working late could find the car park poorly lit and their car parked in an isolated spot which makes them vulnerable to attack. An organisation should consider the safety of its staff when designing a car park. Perimeter fencing, CCTV, lighting and gates which prevent unauthorised access could be considered. Car parking spaces reserved for senior staff should not be obviously marked. Patrols of the car park by security officers are also a good deterrent. Staff who may be expected to work late should be able to reserve parking spaces closer to the building.

Some organisations may have a dedicated staff entrance and care should be taken to ensure the safety of staff arriving and leaving work. Protesters and disgruntled individuals may gather at the entrance to physically or verbally abuse staff. The area outside the entrance should be covered by CCTV and security officers should be vigilant to potentially hostile activity. If protesters gather outside, an alternative entrance should be opened for the duration of the protest to allow staff to enter or leave without facing the protesters. Security officers can be present outside an office during certain times to prevent loitering by individuals who may cause a nuisance to staff or visitors.

Smoking areas are often designated outside the organisation's premises. These can provide an opportunity for attackers to verbally abuse or assault staff. Smoking areas should be covered by CCTV with adequate signage to provide a deterrent. Screens can be installed around the smoking area to provide some protection against projectiles thrown at staff and to prevent staff being observed by potential attackers. A telephone or intercom can be fitted to enable staff to alert security officers if they perceive a threat. Staff can be discouraged from using the smoking area during periods of heightened risk, such as a planned demonstration outside the building.

Screening of Visitors and Callers

Another important aspect of workplace security is the screening of visitors and telephone enquiries. Disgruntled individuals may arrive at reception and ask to speak to a member of staff or call the organisation's main contact telephone number. An assessment of the legitimacy of unexpected visitors should be made before they are permitted access past reception. Visitors can be required to make an appointment before they are permitted access to the premises. All calls to the main contact telephone number can be recorded to deter verbal abuse and calls only accepted if caller ID is enabled.

Staff Whereabouts

Organisations should maintain basic awareness of where their staff should be on a daily basis. Staff working away from the office for a period of time should check in periodically or their manager should contact them if they have not heard from them. Staff who are unaccounted for (e.g. do not turn up for work, but have not booked leave or called in sick) should be identified and contact established to make sure they are safe. Initially, this will be done by telephone, but periods of absence greater than two or three days where contact has not been made, should be reported to the human resources department who should visit their home. Their next of kin may also be contacted to confirm that they are safe.

Personal Protective Equipment (PPE)

Some staff may require specialist equipment to preserve their personal safety. Common examples include body armour issued to security officers, events stewards or inspectors. It can also include audible alarms, first aid kits, spit kits (to collect samples of saliva to enable the perpetrators to be more easily identified and prosecuted) and puncture resistant gloves. The organisation should identify the requirements for staff to be issued with PPE and have a policy on its use, inspection, replacement and staff training.

Over-Watch

This is a procedure whereby staff carrying out activities where there is a particular risk to their safety can be supervised by a colleague. A common example is a warehouse guarded by two security officers, one of whom goes on patrol whilst the other follows their progress on CCTV so they can raise the alarm if the patrolling officer is attacked by an intruder. Over-watch can also be carried out remotely. For instance, staff about to carry out a function which may incur a specific threat, such as a key holder responding to an alarm activation, can contact a colleague just before they start the activity. The colleague can contact them after an agreed period of time (e.g. 30 minutes) to make sure they are safe and raise the alarm if they do not get a response after two or three attempts.

Alternate Workplace Security

Some organisations have a corporate headquarters and smaller satellite offices, warehouses, garages or distribution centres. Whist corporate headquarters may be the main focal point for threats against the organisation, especially if they have a high profile, alternate workplaces are also a potential target which cannot be overlooked. Such locations may have fewer staff and the organisation may not consider it cost effective to invest in substantial security measures. With few staff on site, there is also little support immediately available during an attack. Working practices in small offices can also differ from those encountered in main offices. Fire doors can be propped open to enable staff to pop out for a cigarette, gates and doors can be left open to provide easy access, security officers can leave their post to assist staff in bringing in goods and security procedures such as entry screening and patrolling can be neglected. These vulnerabilities can arise in any location, including large corporate headquarters, but alternate workplaces, especially if they are quieter, are more susceptible. These lax practices can expose staff to physical and verbal assault.

In addition to the security controls described under the previous heading, there are additional security controls that can be employed at alternate workplaces.

Random Site Visits

Random visits to site can be undertaken by a security patrol to provide a deterrent to potential attackers observing the site. To be effective, patrols need to do more than drive up to the site and back to their permanent base. Patrol officers should get out of their vehicle, make contact with staff, check entry points and inspect the perimeter.

Escorts During Vulnerable Hours

The periods at the beginning and end of the working day or shift are most vulnerable for staff locking or unlocking the site. A security escort can be provided during these times to ensure staff can enter and leave the site safely.

Minimum Staffing Requirements

This ensures that an alternate workplace must have a minimum number of staff to function safely. If staffing falls below this level (e.g. due to sickness absence), additional staff may be brought in to cover the shortfall or the site may be closed until the next shift or working day.

Centrally Monitored CCTV

A central control room in a main building could have access to the CCTV footage from the alternate workplace to enable security officers to supervise staff.

Personal Communications

Staff may be required to work alone for long periods of time. For example, there may be only two security officers on duty during a shift at a warehouse which is closed at night. One officer may carry out a patrol whilst the other remains in the control room. If the patrolling officer discovers a trespasser, they have little support. Staff working alone can be provided with a radio with an alarm button linked to a central control room to alert others than they are in danger. Alternatively, an alert tag, such as a fob attached to a lanyard they can wear around their neck which can transmit an alert signal at the press of a button if they are in danger.

Periodic Check-In

A supervisor or manager can check-in with staff periodically to ensure they are OK. Regular radio checks with security officers on lone guard posts can be used to verify they are safe. A covert duress code can also be employed so the security officer can alert their supervisors if they are in danger.

External Events

External events include work-related functions such as meetings, conferences, trade fairs and presentations. Where they are run by the organisation, the risks are easier to manage as the organisation can exert some control over the venues and external staff (e.g. caterers, entertainment and venue facilities staff). However, some events may be run by other companies which may not appreciate the security concerns of all the organisations involved. Some events may be large and widely advertised, but have little public interest. Others may attract widespread public attention and large crowds may arrive to watch the proceedings.

If the organisation is responsible for running an event, it should consider the following security measures:

a. **risk assessment:** the first stage is to conduct a risk assessment to identify potential threats and vulnerabilities;

b. **security plan:** this describes how the risks will be mitigated and describe security measures, protocols and emergency procedures;

c. **security services:** the organisation must decide whether it has the capacity within its own security department to provide guarding, patrolling and other security services for an event or whether it should hire a security contractor;

d. **pre-briefing:** whether the organisation provides its own security staff or relies on a contractor, it should ensure all security, and other events staff, are briefed on the security plan;

e. **supervision:** even the best made plans rarely succeed without deviation. On-site supervision and management is required to respond to unforeseen eventualities and ensure the security plan is implemented effectively. Part of the supervision process will usually involve maintaining a log of actions and decisions throughout the event. This is an important record for post-incident investigation and de-brief; and

f. **de-briefing:** the security aspects of the event should be discussed afterwards to enable lessons to be learned and applied for future events.

Where an event is run by another company, there are some important measures the organisation may wish to take to ensure the security of its staff.

Security Liaison

The event organisers may have their own internal security department managing the event or may hire a contractor to fulfil this role. Whatever the case, it is important that the organisation's security department liaises with them early on in the process and keeps in contact throughout. A good relationship between the parties is vital in ensuring information is passed on and a frank and open dialogue is established. The organisation should pass on details of any known troublemakers to the event security team to ensure they can keep a lookout for them.

Advance Reconnaissance

The organisation's security department can undertake a reconnaissance of the venue prior to the event taking place. This will enable them to see the security measures for themselves and assess whether they are sufficient or whether additional measures should be discussed with the events management team.

Security Presence

The organisation's security team may be present at the event so they can provide assistance if required. This may amount to no more than one security adviser on hand who can contact the event security team to request updates on any incidents, request support and ask for minor modifications to the security plan to cope with unforeseen eventualities. It may also include a security team to protect the organisation's staff.

Emergency Plan

The organisation may wish to develop its own emergency plan for its staff should a serious incident occur during an event. This can include evacuating its staff or finding a safe place at the event to keep them for a short time whilst an incident is assessed. Such a plan must be discussed with the event organisers to ensure it does not conflict with their own emergency procedures.

Home Security

This is a difficult area for the organisation to establish, monitor and enforce security controls as it is usually outside its authority. This is particularly challenging when staff rent accommodation and share it with other lodgers.

Security Advice

Staff can be provided with basic security advice and local police forces sometimes produce helpful booklets and leaflets which the organisation can distribute to its staff. This can include guidance on securing the property, dealing with callers, and responding to harassment. Staff at particular risk can be provided with professional security advice. This can include a security survey of their home and a written report highlighting potential vulnerabilities.

Physical Security Measures

The installation of security measures at a member of staff's home can be a very sensitive issue as many physical security controls, which may be routine in the workplace, will be unacceptable. Some residences may be shared with other people (e.g. spouses, children, lodgers, or co-habitants) who may not have a similar security concern to the member of staff requiring protection. Security controls can also increase the profile of a residence and highlight the sensitivity of the occupant to neighbours and casual callers. Security measures installed at residences must be carefully considered and their value must be weighed against their potential impact on the life of the member of staff and other occupants. Typical security controls could include discreet use of CCTV, intruder alarms, door entry phone, double glazing with a high standard of security and sturdy external doors with multiple locking points. Another feature which could be installed, but is less common, is a strong room or keep (sometimes referred to as a panic room) where occupants can take refuge during an attack. These can be highly engineered with a bullet resistant shell, CCTV monitoring, filtered air supply, back-up generator and supplies of food and equipment. However, they can also be much simpler. A room in a house could be designated as a keep and have a reinforced door and frame fitted and a kitbag kept inside with essential supplies (e.g. mobile phone and charger/adaptor to ensure those inside can call for help). Staff considered to be at high risk of attack may have a large residence requiring more extensive protection, including a perimeter barrier, access control and on-site guards. The safeguarding of rubbish is also an important security measures as hostile groups often search rubbish bins to look for sensitive documents. All documents, work-related and private, must be shredded before disposal. Staff may also wish to consider the implications of other types of waste being recovered. For instance, waste from medicines can indicate a health problem which a hostile group could use to exert pressure. Discarded clothing could also be taken and used to claim the individual was somewhere they should not have been.

Funding for Security Measures

Security measures can be expensive, especially for an individual to finance. An organisation should have clear policies on what funding is available for improving the security of staff residences considered at risk because of the nature of their work. Another issue is what happens to the security measures when the member of staff leaves employment with the organisation. The organisation must be clear on what it will do with the measures it has funded, such as recover them so they can be deployed elsewhere or simply write them off.

Callers and Visitors

Threat groups can sometimes pose as legitimate visitors such as police officers claiming a right to enter and search the property, utility companies checking meters, or fire service staff checking smoke alarms. Staff must be wary of such callers and ensure they check for identification and, if necessary, check with their employer. If staff have any concerns, they should not open the door to the caller and refuse them access.

Temporary Accommodation

Staff may find themselves the focus of hostile actions for a limited period of time due to the nature of their work. For example, during strike action, hostile news coverage or court cases. The homes of staff may already be known to potential attackers or they could be followed home from work. They may then be subject to harassment and intimidation including people calling at the house late at night, access to their property barred, or verbal abuse each time they enter or leave. In such instances, staff can be provided with hotel accommodation away from their home, to limit their exposure to verbal and physical attacks. The identity and location of the hotel must be kept confidential as the safety of staff will depend on potential attackers not knowing its location. This does not prevent the homes of staff being attacked, but at least it will prevent direct intimidation and harassment.

Leisure

An individual's leisure activities pose a particular security challenge as they will naturally want to relax, forget about the pressures of their work and interact with new people they may not know well. This presents a potential avenue of attack for a hostile party seeking to build a relationship with the individual which they can exploit.

Personal Information

Some sports clubs, societies, social groups or professional institutes require personal information to be submitted as part of the subscription process. This can involve details such as home address, employer, medical details and payment information (e.g. credit card details). Professional institutes in particular, may also produce a membership directory where some information will be shared with its members. Potentially this could compromise personal information which could be of use to a hostile party. Staff should be warned of the dangers of sharing such information and informed what details they should not share with bodies outside work. They may argue that no-one outside work knows anything about their organisation, but hostile groups will carry out research on target staff and will seek to get closer to them in a leisure environment. Where staff have any concerns about the requirements for bodies outside work to gather personal information, they should contact their security unit for further advice. Cover details, such as a postal address different from their residential address, may be provided or some details omitted from registration forms.

Dealing with Suspicious Approaches

Staff may be approached by individuals in a leisure environment who seek to exploit such contact for malicious purposes. Examples include building a personal relationship, luring them to a location where they can be attacked, involving them in a compromising situation or gaining information which can be used to attack the organisation. Staff should be made aware of the threat of suspicious approaches and should be provided with a brief description of triggers to watch out for, including:

a.   individuals with a greater knowledge of staff or their work than they would be expected to have;

b.   individuals who seem particularly interested in staff, but no-one else in the social setting;

c.   individuals who are unusually assertive or persistent that staff go somewhere with them or meet them again; and

d.   individuals who keep close to staff, but do not attempt to interact with them, such as avoiding eye contact or not exchanging pleasantries.

This is not an exhaustive list of suspicious behaviour, but provides an indication of the signs staff should be aware of. Staff who experience suspicious approaches should report them to the security unit. Usually, there is little that can be done to address individual cases, but a number of reports of suspicious approaches can highlight trends such as particular venues (e.g. bars or coffee shops around the organisation's premises), staff who may be under surveillance by hostile parties or individuals who are taking an interest in the organisation.

Discussing Sensitive Information

A common vulnerability in the leisure environment is that staff socialising outside work often talk about their work as it is one of the few things a number of colleagues will have in common. This can result in sensitive information being disclosed to outside parties. There is little that can reasonably be done to prevent staff talking about their work, but they can be made aware of issues that should not be discussed in public, irrespective or how discreet they think they are. The organisation can provide a 'no-speak' or 'don't speak' list to their staff of issues they must not discuss in public. These can include:

   a. any issue which is the subject of current or potential legal proceedings;

   b. disciplinary action against staff;

   c. security incidents;

   d. controversial areas of work;

   e. current tenders or contract negotiations; and

   f. breaches of regulatory or contractual obligations.

Such practices can protect the organisation as a whole, but are specifically designed to prevent staff being targeted by hostile parties because of their employment. They may be followed out of a bar and attacked or attempts made to involve them in compromising situations so they can be pressured to reveal sensitive information or facilitate access to the organisation's premises.

Online Profile

Staff should be aware of their online profile and ensure they understand the vulnerabilities this may have. Chatrooms, blogs, message boards and social networking sites provide opportunities to meet new people with similar interests or professions and share information and ideas. However, these generate a number of potential vulnerabilities. Staff may give away more information about themselves and their employment than they intend when working online from their home where they feel comfortable and safe. Staff may be targeted by online bullying, either because of their work, associations with others or aspects of their personal life. Staff may make inappropriate or offensive comments believing that they are doing so privately and 'off-the-record' which may generate negative public and press attention for the organisation. It is important staff are briefed on these vulnerabilities and provided with basic online security advice. This can include:

a. maintain good security of personal IT systems, including passwords and virus protection;

b. be aware of approaches by strangers online, particularly if they seem to know more about the individual or their work than they should do;

c. keep their professional and personal lives separate online by using separate e-mail addresses, mobile numbers and telephone numbers for work and personal use, not providing details of work on personal forums and not providing details of personal life on professional forums; and

d. warn family and friends not to disclose professional information of staff in their own online profile.

Safeguarding the Organisation's Assets

Staff sometimes travel to leisure activities direct from work and may have sensitive assets with them such as access passes, documents or laptops. Hostile parties sometimes follow staff to leisure activities where they can be robbed. Staff may be seriously injured to prevent them immediately informing their organisation of such losses, such as access passes which can be used before they are deactivated. Staff should be informed of the risks of taking sensitive assets with them to leisure activities and reminded to keep them safe and preferably out of sight.

Vulnerable Situations

Some social situations will expose staff to high levels of personal risk. An example is staff becoming intoxicated in a busy city centre late on a Saturday evening. They may be incapable of looking after themselves, they may become separated from friends and may be subject to assault by drunken revellers or targeted by hostile groups. Obviously it is up to staff what they do in their private life and the organisation can exert little control over their actions. However, it may wish to provide staff with general information on their safety which can be found on websites of police departments, councils and victim support groups.

Business Travel

Business travel includes staff travelling while at work, the CEO travelling to a major public event, a lorry driver transporting valuable goods, Cash In Transit (CIT) drivers transporting money or the organisation's lawyer travelling to a meeting with sensitive documents.

Professional Drivers

Some organisations rely on professional drivers for business travel, either employed directly by the organisation or contracted from a chauffeur company. They can be trained with skills to improve the security of business travel such as searching the vehicle before departure, route planning, keeping the vehicle secure when not in use, defensive driving skills, anti-surveillance techniques and first aid skills.

Defensive Driving Training

An alternative to using professional drivers, is to train staff with defensive driving techniques to enhance their current driving skills. This can provide them with better anticipation and awareness and help them respond appropriately to an attack, such as an attempt to force their vehicle to stop, attempts to gain access to a stationary vehicle and attempts to cause their vehicle to crash.

Secure Transport

The organisation can install physical security measures to its vehicles, or hire vehicles with such measures already installed. One example is a Cash In Transit (CIT) van, sometimes called an armoured car, which is custom built with substantial physical protection. Lorries can be fitted with CCTV cameras to detect and record attempted robberies and have locks, retaining cables and security seals fitted to the load compartment.

Tracking and Monitoring

Vehicles can be fitted with electronic systems to track their progress and automatically report their location and travel to a central monitoring station. The organisation can monitor such systems itself or contract a service from a specialist company. This can provide a deterrent against hijacking and can help locate a vehicle that has been seized. Such systems can also include a personal alarm which the occupants of a vehicle can use to signal that they are under attack.

Overnight Stops

Vehicles which stop overnight are vulnerable to being robbed of any cargo they are carrying. Staff who remain with the vehicle are also in danger of being attacked. Drivers of lorries which are empty often leave the back doors to the load compartment open overnight so potential robbers can see there is nothing worth taking. Route planning can identify safer places to stop where CCTV is in operation and other people are present to raise the alarm if they witness an attack. For example, a designated truck-stop or motorway services are better locations than a layby or a back road on an industrial estate. The best option, where possible, is for transport to be planned so that overnight stops are not necessary.

Close Protection Officers

Close Protection Officers (CPO) are individuals trained to provide protection to persons at risk of physical attack. They can operate individually or as part of a

Close Protection Team (CPT). They can be allocated to a specific individual or work in a pool accessible by a number of staff, as required. This is probably one of the costliest and disruptive forms of personal security and is usually reserved for extremely high levels of threat. A wealthy CEO of an organisation may use CPOs either permanently or during public events or other occasions when they are at higher risk. Other staff may also require CPOs for limited periods, for instance if they are investigators or lawyers of the organisation involved in legal proceedings and may be subject to threats and intimidation when travelling to pre-trial proceedings or court appearances. Few organisations will have their own in-house CPOs and most will contract such a service from a professional close protection company.

Personal Travel

Personal travel is a vulnerable point in an individual's pattern of life as they are outside the protective environments of their home or work place and interact with large volumes of people in public. Personal travel can also set a predictable pattern of times and routes between home and work or regular leisure activities. Ideally staff at risk of hostile action should vary their travel plans to avoid setting a pattern, but realistically few staff will want to maintain such an inconvenience for very long and would only do so for a limited period of time if they believed a specific threat existed. There are some basic security procedures staff can observe during personal travel.

Situational Awareness

Whichever mode of travel staff use, they must always maintain awareness of their surroundings to identify if they are subject to unwelcome attention or potential hostility. Staff should not become paranoid and look for threats at every turn, but should be aware when something is different from what they normally experience.

Private Transport

Staff can be provided with basic security guidance when driving their own vehicle, such as keeping valuables out of site, ensuring all car doors are locked and windows raised and keep a gap of at least one car length from the vehicle in front when stationary to avoid being boxed-in. Enhanced vehicle security advice may also be required for staff at particular risk of criminal or terrorist attack. Searching the vehicle before getting in, keeping it in a locked garage, learning to recognise signs of tampering or sabotage and anti-surveillance driving techniques may be required.

Public Transport

This is obviously a more vulnerable mode of travel than private transport as staff have contact with large numbers of people in an environment they cannot control. The organisation can provide its staff with basic security guidance on travelling on public transport which it can obtain from open source information such as police websites. There are some obvious points staff should be aware of such as never use unlicensed mini-cabs, avoid using public transport late in the evening or early hours of the morning. If staff have to travel during these times they should sit close to the driver so they can raise the alarm if they feel threatened. Maintaining awareness on public transport is much harder than private transport. Staff do not have to pay attention when someone else is in control and may either read a book, listen to music or take a nap. This will reduce their awareness and inhibit their reaction time if they are attacked or threatened.

Reporting Unusual Events

Staff can note any unusual events they encounter when travelling and report it to their organisation if it is repeated more than two or three times. This will help the organisation develop better security advice for its staff. For instance, a number of staff may report suspicious activity on public transport around the workplace, such as approaches from strangers, the same person paying close attention to them or hostility from protesters or activists. The organisation may provide advice on avoiding certain routes or times and involve the police if they feel such actions may constitute harassment.

Further Reading

Alston.H and Beckford.C: Home Security (2005); New Holland Publishers Ltd

Bazell.M: Personal Digital Security – Protecting Yourself from Online Crime (2013); CreateSpace Independent Publishing Platform

Bennett.R: Workplace Violence Solutions: A Step-by-Step Guide to a Safer Workplace (2013); CreateSpace Independent Publishing Platform

Godesen.R: Personal Security Pocket Book (2014); Military Pocket Books

Honey.G: Complete Home Security Guide, The (2012); Crowood Press Ltd

Payne.T: Home Secuirty – Protecting your Home from Burglary (2012); CreateSpace Independent Publishing Platform

Robbins.C: Understanding Personal Data Security (2015); Middle Class Tech

Smith.E: Workplace Security Essentials - A Guide for Helping Organizations Create Safe Work Environments (2014); Butterworth Heinemann

3.4
Information Security

The aim of information security is to prevent unauthorised access or interference to information assets.

Its objectives are:

    a. **confidentiality:** to ensure only authorised users have access to information for legitimate purposes;

    b. **integrity:** to ensure information is maintained in a complete and accurate form; and

    c. **availability:** to ensure information can be accessed by authorised users whenever required.

Information security, or INFOSEC as it is often abbreviated, is an umbrella term for three closely-related fields: IT security, communications security and document security.

These three subjects have become interlinked because IT systems are the foundation for communications and documentation, which is commonly produced, stored and distributed on IT systems. However, there are also communications and documentation which are processed outside of IT systems such as telephones, faxes, filing systems and pre-printed forms. Therefore, whilst these three fields closely interact, they also have elements that exist separately. This web of overlapping controls is shown in Figure 10: Scope of Information Security. There is a danger that an organisation will focus on the IT aspects of information security. However, once a user prints a document in hard copy, the information has now left the scope of IT-centric information policy.

When producing an information security policy, there are three approaches which can be adopted:

    a. produce a single policy covering IT, communications and document security;

    b. produce separate policies for each area and clearly define their parameters; or

    c. produce a technical security policy covering IT systems, and areas where it overlaps communications and document security, but separate policies where these areas stand alone.

Whichever approach is adopted, it is important to ensure that all elements in the information security model are covered.

Figure 10: Scope of Information Security

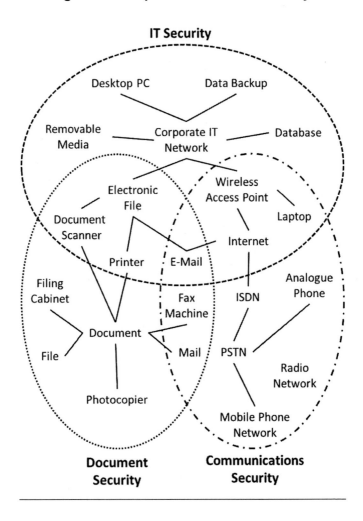

Further Reading

Alexander.D, Finch.A, Sutton.D and Taylor.A:
Information Security Management Principles (2013);
BCS, The Chartered Institute for IT

Andress.J: Basics of Information Security, The (2011);
Syngress

O'Hanley. R and Tiller.J: Information Security
Management Handbook (2013); Auerbach
Publications

Peltier.T: Information Security Policies and
Procedures: A Practitioner's Reference, Second
Edition: Guidelines for Effective Information Security
Management (2004); Auerbach Publications

Raggad.B: Information Security Management:
Concepts and Practice (2010); CRC Press

Rhodes-Ousley.M: Information Security – The
Complete Reference (2013); McGraw Hill Osborne

Wheeler.E: Security Risk Management – Building an
Information Security Risk Management Program from
the Ground Up (2011); Syngress

3.5
IT Security

The aim of IT security is to prevent unauthorised access or interference to IT systems and processes.

The objectives are:

a. **access:** to ensure only authorised users have access to IT systems, or specific aspects of them, for legitimate purposes;

b. **authenticity:** to ensure the validity of individuals, system components and processes carried out on IT systems;

c. **alteration:** to prevent unauthorised damage, destruction or modification to IT systems; and

d. **appropriate use:** to ensure authorised individuals use IT systems only for approved purposes.

Examples of specific threats to information security include:

a. **intrusion:** unauthorised access to an organisation's IT system;

b. **abuse of access rights:** unauthorised actions carried out by an authorised user;

c. **information disclosure:** unauthorised access to information;

d. **process corruption:** causing an IT system to carry out a process incompletely or incorrectly;

e. **repudiation:** denying that a particular function was carried out; and

f. **denial of service:** preventing access to IT systems for authorised users.

Intrusion is access to an IT system by an unauthorised user, which is commonly referred to as 'hacking'. They can be individuals outside the organisation or one of its own staff who are attempting to gain access to systems to which they are not authorised. Intrusion can be carried out purely for its own sake, and many hackers do it for the challenge of breaching security controls. However, it can also be carried out as a precursor to mounting other forms of attack, such as information disclosure or process corruption.

Abuse of access rights occurs when users exploit their authorised access for unauthorised purposes. This can include accessing personal details of staff or clients for illegitimate reasons, sending offensive or derogatory e-mails to colleagues or external contacts or excessive personal use of IT systems. Such incidents can adversely affect the working relationship between staff, can damage client confidence and incur legal liability.

Information disclosure can occur unintentionally through the careless handling of information. A common example occurs when staff forward an e-mail chain to an individual without realising they are not entitled to see the full content. Minor disclosure of information is often called 'seepage' and each disclosure is not necessarily damaging. However, a number of disclosures can result in a large quantity of information being collected by target groups over a period of time. Disclosures can be external (ie to parties outside the organisation) or internal (ie to staff within the organisation who are not entitled to have access to the information). External disclosures are potentially more damaging, but internal disclosures can affect staff relations and cause disruption which can impede the organisation's efficiency.

Information disclosure occurs when confidential information is released to unauthorised individuals. The information may not be stolen in a way that other assets are, but the very fact that others now have access to it may cause damage to the organisation. For instance, sensitive information on an organisation's bids for a tender may disadvantage it when it competes with other organisations for the contract. The disclosure of personal information on staff may cause embarrassment, incur legal liability and adversely affect staff morale.

One of the greatest challenges in responding to the threat of information disclosure is that it is not always obvious who has access to the information and what they intend to do with it. Some information may get no further than a hacker's waste bin, whilst others may fall into the hands of criminal groups. Unless the organisation discovers who has its information and for what purpose, it must assume the worst.

Process corruption occurs when an IT system functions in a way other than what was intended. It can occur as a result of user error (e.g. entering inaccurate or incomplete data) or by altering an IT system's operating protocols. There are a number of ways this can be caused, including viruses, improper setup and installation of software or unauthorised changes to operating systems.

Repudiation occurs when an individual claims that a particular function was not carried out, in whole or in part. For example, denying that a particular e-mail was sent or received or claiming that an action purportedly carried out by them was actually carried out by someone else. This can have legal consequences when an organisation attempts to enforce contract conditions it claims another party has failed to meet.

Denial of Service (DoS) attacks prevent authorised individuals using a system, either permanently or temporarily. A Distributed Denial of Service (DDoS) attack involves a number of DoS attacks from different sources. Such attacks are often carried out by protesters or disgruntled individuals seeking to cause disruption to the target organisation. DoS and DDoS attacks commonly focus on sites or services based on web servers which can be publicly accessed. Most attacks are only temporary, but an organisation which relies on its web server to do business can lose substantial sums of money before services are resumed.

The concept of IT security controls can be represented as a series of layers, each performing a separate, but related security function. This is shown in Figure 11: IT Security Model, which shows a simple IT network.

Fig.11: IT Security Model

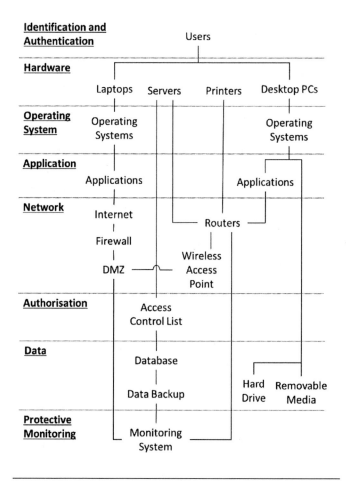

Identification and Authentication

Identification and authentication is a process by which authorised users gain access to an IT system. There are two elements to this process:

    a. **identification:** the user enters their credentials, usually a user name and password, into the system; and

    b. **authentication:** the IT system verifies the details are correct and provides access.

Identification and authentication controls may include the following:

User Registration

This is a procedure to allow new users to gain access to the IT system. It involves a formal request, usually provided by completing an application form, submitted to the system administrators asking them to set up an IT account for the individual. The request should identify the individual (their name, date of birth, employee number and the unit they are working in) and state why they require access. For new entrants to the organisation, the request could originate from the human resources section when the individual is recruited and provided with a start date to join. Some organisations may allow other parties, such as contractors or consultants, to have access to their IT systems. They will also require a formal registration to be submitted. A sponsor may be required to justify why a new user requires access. With new entrants, this is straightforward and a simple explanation that they are new staff is all that is required. For third parties, this may involve a brief statement from a manager in a business unit they are working with to explain why they need access. This is important for post-incident analysis when a third party misuses their access rights and the organisation must establish why they were provided access in the first place. User registration documentation should be retained on record for as long as the user has access to the IT system.

Acceptable Use Policy

This describes what the organisation considers to be acceptable use of its IT network and highlights conduct it considers unacceptable. An organisation may permit reasonable personal use of its IT network, including the Internet and e-mail system. Unacceptable use may include:

a. accessing inappropriate material on the Internet;

b. sending or forwarding e-mails which include profane or offensive content;

c. breaching confidentiality of staff, customers or clients;

d. disclosing sensitive information belonging to the organisation or its stakeholders;

e. sending or forwarding e-mails with content which breaches copyright;

f. furthering personal interests, or those of another party; and

g. incurring costs (e.g. subscriptions or pay for access services) which the organisation will be charged for.

Users should be required to complete a declaration stating that they have read and understood the organisation's acceptable use policy as part of, or soon after, the user registration process. This can be done electronically when they first log onto the organisation's IT network.

Privilege Management

This describes what resources a user is permitted access to. The principle often applied is 'least privilege', which means a user should only have the minimum access required to perform their role. The IT section will normally have a list of what resources should routinely be given to all new users, including the organisation's intranet, e-mail system and basic software packages. Access to any additional resources would require a formal request from the business unit where the user works or the asset owner who is responsible for the resource. Privileges which are additional to the basic level available to all system users must be regularly reviewed to ensure the user has an ongoing requirement to retain them. It is a common problem that users provided with access rights required in a specific job do not relinquish them when they move to another post within the organisation.

Password Management

Whilst biometrics and tokens could be used to provide access to an IT system, passwords are the most common form of access credential. Where passwords are used, the following security controls should apply:

a. **password strength:** the number and type of characters required for a password should be specified by the IT system. Passwords will normally include a minimum of 6-8 characters, including at least one upper and lower case letter, one number and one symbol. Passwords which do not meet this requirement should not be accepted by the IT system.

b. **password expiry:** passwords should only be used for a limited period of time before the user is required to change them (e.g. 90 days). The next password should not be similar to the last one. For instance, some users will try to use the same password but with a sequential number at the end which they will amend when required to change their password. This is too predictable and the IT system should be able to recognise similar passwords and reject them.

c. **unique passwords:** each user should have their own password which is known only by them. No password should ever be shared between more than one user.

d. **written records:** users should memorise their passwords and not write them down. However, staff may have several passwords and PIN codes to remember for business and personal IT systems and cannot reasonably be expected to remember them all. Therefore, it is inevitable that they will have to write them down somewhere, at least until they are familiar with them. Passwords written down must be kept secure and, if they are compromised, must be changed as soon as possible. Common hiding places for notes of passwords include under keyboards, on the back of monitors and under desks. Such practices should be discouraged.

Unattended Equipment

Individuals must lock-out their IT equipment when they are away from their desk to prevent someone else using their system. This prevents other staff gaining access to data and applications they may not be authorised to use. It also prevents staff carrying out actions that the system logs will record against another individual's user name.

Automatic Lock-Out and Log-Out

IT systems which have been inactive for a certain period of time (e.g. more than 5-10 minutes) should automatically lock-out which enables the screensaver and requires the password to be entered to unlock it. This ensures that someone attempting to gain access to unattended equipment a user has omitted to lock-out themselves only has a limited period of time to do so. When IT equipment has been left unattended for a very long time it should automatically log-out which shuts down completely. This ensures that equipment left running when the user goes home, still runs a shutdown sequence and installs and updates software.

Hardware

Hardware is the IT equipment itself and includes PCs, servers, printers, switches, routers and all cabling and connections. Hardware security controls are designed to prevent unauthorised interference to this equipment, including theft and damage.

Asset Register

This is a document (frequently stored electronically) or a database which records every item of IT equipment the organisation is responsible for, including:

    a.   identifying features such as make, model, serial number and any asset number the organisation has allocated;

    b.   the date it was installed on the organisation's premises;

    c.   the location where it is installed or, if it is mobile equipment such as a laptop, the location where it is normally stored; and

    d.   the asset owner (ie the individual responsible for the asset).

Physical Protection

Physical measures can be installed to prevent unauthorised access or interference to IT equipment. Servers should be located in a secure room with adequate doors, locks and access control systems to prevent unauthorised access. Intruder alarm systems and CCTV should also be installed. Local switches and routers should be housed in secure containers or cupboards. Individual items of IT equipment can be fitted with retaining devices which prevent unauthorised removal, such as a steel cable attached to a surface such as a wall, floor or desk. PCs can be fitted with removable hard drives which can be locked away in a cupboard at the end of the working day. Lockable panels can be fitted to power-on buttons or removable media drives and ports.

Labelling and Marking

IT equipment can often be bought in many retail outlets and it is not always possible for the organisation to identify its own if the manufacturer's label containing the serial number is removed. This can cause a problem when identifying lost or stolen equipment or if an IT contractor finishes its contract with the organisation and wishes to remove its own equipment from the organisation's premises. IT equipment can be labelled to clearly indicate that it belongs to the organisation. Such labelling can include the company's name and logo, an office address and asset number. Covert marking can also be used to help identify IT equipment which has been stolen and had all other identifying features removed. Such marking can include watermarks, ultra-violet ink and electronic tags which are not visible to the naked eye. Specific component parts which have a high value can also be individually marked in case stolen IT equipment is broken down for its parts.

Cabling Protection

The cabling which connects IT equipment to a network can be protected from unauthorised physical interference such as attaching it to unauthorised equipment, cutting it, or removing a portion of the outer cover to enable unauthorised connections to be made. Cabling is often made easily accessible for IT engineers in drop ceilings, wall mounted trunking or under floor tiles. Therefore, it can be vulnerable to unauthorised interference. Trunking can be made from metal or tough plastic and have removable sections which are locked using a universal key issued only to a limited number of IT engineers. Lockable clamps are also available which fit onto the back of IT equipment so that cabling cannot be removed and connected to unauthorised equipment.

Electrical Supply Protection

IT equipment can be damaged or disabled by fluctuations in the electrical supply. This can be mitigated by measures installed in the organisation's electrical plant room. Access to the electrical plant room must be restricted to authorised persons only and a good level of physical security installed (including doors, locks, intruder alarms and CCTV) to prevent unauthorised access. To protect IT equipment from power failure, a UPS (Uninterrupted Power Supply) system can be installed which ensures power can be supplied locally in the event of a power cut. This often includes a generator of sufficient size to meet the organisation's basic electrical supply needs. However, this will take time to start up and IT processes and data can be corrupted if they lose power for any period of time. A battery backup can be used to bridge the gap between a loss of power and initialisation of a generator. These batteries can either be stored in the electrical plant room or attached to individual items of equipment.

Operating System

An operating system is a program which tells the computer how it should operate when it is switched on. It controls the hardware the computer is attached to (e.g. mouse, keyboard and monitor) the data drives (e.g. hard disk, CD ROM drive, and USB drives) and network connections. It can also schedule tasks the computer performs routinely. Security controls can be applied to each computer's operating system to ensure it functions securely and does not permit activities which may cause harm to the organisation's IT system.

Pre-Boot Authentication (PBA)

Also known as Power-On Authentication (POA), this requires the user to enter their user name and password before anything is read from the hard disk. This prevents any form of access to applications or data before the user's identity has been verified.

Administrator Access

Administrator accounts have wide ranging permissions to change how the operating system is set up and configured and what permissions it allows different users. Normal users of the system should not be set up with administrator accounts and their permissions should not allow them to make changes to the operating system. Those with administrator accounts should be kept to a minimum number of authorised IT engineers.

Default Accounts

Operating systems can have generic user accounts with standard passwords installed by the manufacturer. These often have wide ranging permissions which allow the operating system to be setup and configured as the user requires. These accounts, including the passwords are often available on the internet and hackers can use them to gain unauthorised access to the organisation's IT system. Therefore, it is important that all default user accounts are either deleted, or the user names and passwords changed, before the equipment is installed or connected to the network.

Drive Connections

The operating system will connect to the available drives when it starts up. These connections can be managed to prevent access to certain drives or to limit such access to authorised activities. For example, the organisation may not permit access to removable media drives (e.g. CD ROM drive) to ensure data cannot be copied to them and prevent viruses being uploaded to the system. The drives could be removed and a blank plate fitted over the port, but the operating system would still recognise the drive if a new one was fitted. Therefore, the operating system can be configured so it will not recognise any drive which is connected to it. Alternatively, the permissions the operating system could allow to the drive could be limited to read-only and not read-and-write access. This would enable data to be viewed and copied from media in the drive but not saved to it.

Unessential Services

Operating systems often have a number of services which allow information to be shared, the internal clock to be synchronised, devices to be located, network connections to be established, registration documentation to be sent to the manufacturer and external support services to be accessed. Not all of these services are required by the organisation and can provide a potential avenue of attack. The organisation must determine which of these services are required and ensure those which are not are disabled.

Executable Space Protection

Portions of a computer's memory are used to run the operating system and space in this memory can be used to run malicious code. Executable space protection is where this redundant space is marked as non-executable which prevents any program or malicious code being run from it. This involves hardware controls built into the Central Processing Unit (CPU) chip and software controls programmed into the operating system.

Anti-Malware

These are programmes which detect and prevent malicious code. They function on the IT network, but can also be installed on the operating system to filter malware from incoming and outgoing traffic. As well as installing anti-malware, the organisation must ensure it is continually updated as new versions are introduced to counter new threats.

Application

An application is software which enables a computer to perform a function beyond the running of the computer itself. Organisations may have many applications available to different users across its IT system and must install, configure and manage them appropriately.

Authorisation

Only authorised applications should be installed on the organisation's IT system. A formal request should be made when a new application needs to be installed (usually a form is completed describing the application and why it is needed). A list of individuals with authorisation to approve the installation of new applications should be maintained. The formal approval to install a new application should be retained on record for future reference, usually on the same form as the request was made. The unauthorised installation of new or modified applications should be regarded as a serious disciplinary offence.

Register of Approved Applications

The organisation should maintain a register of applications available on its IT system, including its name, the company which produced it, a brief description of what it does, the most recent version number and details of any patching or modification which has been carried out. It should also record where the application is stored (e.g. the identity of the server or computers where it is installed). This makes it easier to identify individual applications if a vulnerability has been identified which requires it to be uninstalled or modified. It also helps identify unauthorised applications which may have been installed.

System Source Code

Applications must only be installed if they have been provided by a reliable source. This prevents rogue editions of applications being installed with malicious or missing segments of code. Normally this is relatively straightforward and the organisation will purchase software, and the licence to use it, direct from the manufacturer. However, this becomes less straightforward when an individual considers downloading an application from the internet, particularly if it is 'shareware' (ie freely available without requiring a user licence). This may seem a good idea as the application can be installed in minutes free of charge. This poses the risk that the software contains malicious code or programming errors which may cause it to behave unpredictably or is unsupported and patches and updates will not be available. The organisation should ensure it sources its applications from reliable companies.

Configuration Management

This defines how an application's settings are configured. The organisation should first consider how it wishes to use the application and what functionality it requires. This will enable a configuration template to be produced which lists the standard settings. Functions which are not required should be disabled.

Identification and Verification

Not everyone who has access to the organisation's IT system will require access to every application on it. Some applications will require identification and verification of users (e.g. by entering a user name and password) before the application can be accessed. In such instances, the same security controls for identification and verification described earlier should be used. However, users to the IT system will already have entered their credentials when they first accessed their computer and entering separate credentials for each application they require is time consuming and frustrating. Therefore, Single Sign-On (SSO) can be employed whereby the user logs-in to their computer once and their credentials are stored so they can be recalled by each application when the user accesses them.

Default User Accounts

Applications which require individual log-in will often have default accounts set up, typically with extensive privileges. All default accounts must be identified, as there may be more than one, and either deleted or have their default settings changed so that they are attributed to a specific individual.

Session Management

A session is a period of continual access of an application by a user and includes the requests for data made by the user and the responses provided by the system. Session management controls can include:

    a. periodic saving of changes so a session can be restored easily if the application ends suddenly;

b. automatically log-out after a period of inactivity;

c. limiting the number of users who can access an application at any one time; and

d. ensuring only one individual can edit a record at any one time, to prevent two individuals making changes which will conflict when the record is saved.

Network

The network is the interconnections between different parts of the organisation's IT system.

Firewalls

These analyse traffic at a point in a network where the level of access changes. The most common point for a firewall is between the organisation's corporate network and the Internet. However, firewalls can also be used internally between different parts of a network which process different levels of sensitive data. A firewall can be configured to block unauthorised or suspicious network traffic by inspecting the packets of data when they pass through it and identifying features which may indicate it includes malware. The effectiveness of a firewall, depends on the extent of its inspection process and the configuration of its blocking protocol.

De-Militarised Zone (DMZ)

This is a combination of security controls which typically include an internal and external firewall either side of a server. The server is usually restricted to a function that requires access to the internet and commonly includes web servers, mail servers, File Transfer Protocol (FTP) servers and Voice over Internet Protocol (VoIP) servers. A DMZ segregates these publicly facing servers from the rest of the network.

Network Intrusion Detection

This is a program which detects suspicious activity on the network. The most common forms are signature based and anomaly based. Signature based detection systems have a database of signatures (ie aspects of different types of attack) which they look for when scanning network traffic. The obvious limitation of this type of intrusion detection is that it may not recognise attacks which are new or are designed to imitate legitimate network traffic. Anomaly based detection systems measure network traffic against a baseline of what would normally be expected to detect unusual patterns. Another limitation with this type of intrusion detection is that legitimate changes in network traffic may trigger false alarms. A larger number of false alarms may obscure suspicious network activity. A combination of network intrusion detection systems is a better solution than relying on a single type. It is also more effective to use separate network intrusion detection systems on different parts of a segregated network. This enables them to scan less traffic more thoroughly and be configured according to the unique aspects of the traffic on the segregated part of the network.

Wireless Connections

These are a particular vulnerability as they may allow anyone in the proximity of a wireless connection to gain access to the network. The organisation may use wireless connections to limit the cabling required to join different parts of the network (e.g. between different buildings on the same site) and unauthorised users in the vicinity may be able to gain access to the network. Staff working remotely (e.g. from a hotel) may use a free local Wi-Fi service which anyone else could also have access to. Sometimes these are password protected, but there is often a single password available to all users of the service. The organisation's wireless connections should require identification and authentication to gain access and can be put on a segregated part of the network behind internal firewalls. A Virtual Private Network (VPN) can be used to provide a secure connection between remote users accessing the organisation's network across the internet. A VPN uses an application installed on the remote terminal to authenticate the user to the network when a connection is established. All traffic subsequently sent through the connection is encrypted.

Equipment Identification

This is where IT equipment is programmed with a unique code which enables it to be identified on the network. This prevents authorised equipment being moved to another part of the network where its use may be prohibited. It also prevents unauthorised equipment being installed which may have capabilities which authorised equipment does not. For example, a printer may be installed in a secure area which has limited memory recall functions. It could be swapped with another printer which has a memory recall enabling the last document sent to it to be printed again. This could enable a member of staff without proper security clearance (e.g. a cleaner or maintenance engineer) to reprint a sensitive document they do not have authorised access to.

Segregation Between Networks

An organisation may have business units which carry out sensitive work that must not be shared with all staff. For instance, the work of the internal audit department or an internal fraud investigation unit may be restricted to limited numbers of authorised staff. In such instances, these units can have their own sub-network segregated from the main corporate system and protected by firewalls and intruder detection systems.

Network Routing Control

This controls the flow of data across a network between the user and the server. A specific route or 'enforced path' can be defined to prevent sensitive data being sent to parts of the network where users do not have authorisation to access it. Network routing controls are commonly encountered in segregated networks and are provided by switching controls and internal firewalls.

Encryption

Network traffic can be encrypted whilst it is travelling across a network. This is particularly useful when IT networks span a number of sites across a Local Area Network (LAN) or Wide Area Network (WAN). It is also useful where a network processes data at varying levels of sensitivity which a restricted number of users have authorised access to. Encryption is a complex subject and detailed analysis is beyond the scope of this publication. A brief overview of cryptography is described in the next section on communications security and the same principles would apply when encrypting data across a network.

Authorisation

Authorisation determines what a user is permitted access to.

Access Control List (ACL)

These are used to control access to parts of an IT system to ensure only authorised users can access it. They usually relate to a specific resource (e.g. a database or file) and define what users are permitted access and under what circumstances. For example, a user may be authorised to have read-only access to a file, but not read-write access. ACLs can also control access to different parts of a network. For instance, a limited number of staff may be able to gain access to a segregated part of the network which processes sensitive information. There are four main methods of compiling an ACL:

   a. **Discretionary Access Control (DAC):** is where an individual, usually the asset owner responsible for the resource, determines who is permitted access and under what circumstances;

   b. **Mandatory Access Control (MAC):** is where a set of rules is established to determine under what circumstances an individual should be provided with access. It may be determined by their level of security clearance or other criteria they must fulfil for access to be granted;

c. **Role Based Access Control (RBAC):** is where an individual's access rights are determined by the role they perform. For example, an individual who works in the finance department may automatically be permitted access to financial records; and

d. **Attribute-Based Access Control (ABAC):** is where specific attributes define what access an individual is permitted, such as time, the location it can be accessed from or the terminals which can access it.

A combination of these methods may also be used and different resources can be managed by different types of access control. There are benefits and limitations to all four methods and the organisation will determine what type of control best suites its IT system and business requirements.

Access Review

Once ACLs have been produced, it is important they are regularly reviewed to ensure an individual's access is still required and they do not retain unnecessary access rights. For instance, an individual may leave the audit department and move to a new post in the finance department. They may be entered on a new ACL for the finance department, but not automatically removed from the ACL for the audit department. Therefore, ACLs must be regularly reviewed to ensure individuals who should have had their access rights removed or restricted have not been overlooked when their access credentials change.

Data

Data controls protect information processed on IT systems from unauthorised interference. It includes all forms of data storage, including hard drives and removable media.

Input Validation

This ensures data has been input completely and accurately into a system. This can be achieved by compulsory fields which must be completed before a record can be saved or by a field providing a limited selection of appropriate data to choose from (e.g. dates saved in a specific format – DD/MM/YYYY). A record cannot be saved until all mandatory fields have been correctly completed. Data fields should also be limited in the amount of information which can be recorded in them to prevent excessive data being input which could corrupt the record.

Data Integrity

This ensures saved data records remain complete and accurate. This can include ensuring any changes to a record follow the same standards as described under 'input validation'. Records which should no longer be changed (e.g. historical finance records or contracts already signed) can be locked to prevent changes being made.

Data Encryption

Data stored anywhere on the IT system should be encrypted to protect it if it is lost or stolen. This includes servers, computer hard drives and removable media.

Data Masking

This conceals certain data within a data set (e.g. a database file) to restrict sensitive information to those required to see it. Some databases may be shared with a large number of users who require access to some, but not all of the data provided. Such fields in a database may be withheld from users with lesser access rights.

Data Erasure

This ensures data that is no longer required is destroyed securely so it cannot be recovered. When data is deleted, it is not immediately wiped from the hard drive, and a digital footprint will remain until that sector of the hard disk is over-written. Data erasure programs can be incorporated into a PC's shutdown sequence to erase this data. If data is encrypted, there will be less of a requirement to do this.

Data Backup

This ensures that data is regularly saved at more than one location. For example, a company may have a server room at its main headquarters where all its data is stored and a backup server at another location where copies of all its data are automatically saved. This ensures that it can still access its data if anything happens to its main server or the data stored on it.

Output Validation

An output is a collection of related data which has been collated at the end of a process. Output validation controls ensures this data is complete and accurate and, in the case of electronic records, does not contain malicious or corrupted code. They can be divided into technical and non-technical controls. Technical controls include scanning records for errors in data fields and malicious or corrupted code. Non-technical controls include recording the search criteria for records in the output document (e.g. a hard copy printout) so errors can be more easily identified.

Protective Monitoring

Protective monitoring is a range of security controls designed to detect unauthorised activity on the IT network.

Vulnerability Monitoring

This is a process to detect and report network services which have known vulnerabilities. This is usually carried out by a software programme which scans ports on the network and determines what services, and versions, are running on them. It will produce a report listing any vulnerabilities it has found including old versions of software, unknown or unauthorised software, or patches not installed.

Network Mapping

This is a process to check the layout of the network to ensure unauthorised changes have not been made. There are a number of software tools to do this which produce a report on the components on a network and the connections between them. Malicious alteration of a network can be carried out by hostile insiders who may install connections to breach a firewall which would otherwise prevent them from gaining access to certain information or installing a wireless access point to enable them to access information remotely. However, it may also be carried out innocently by engineers, particularly contractors, working on the system who may install wireless access points to enable remote monitoring and diagnostic of system performance or alter connections to tidy up a network without understanding why such connections were installed a certain way. Therefore, network mapping is important to ensure network architecture remains as it was originally designed.

Audit Logging

This involves the automated recording of activity on a network to record any unauthorised behaviour. All activity can be logged, but logs will usually be restricted to key information only, including:

    a.   identity of a user on the system (name and staff number);

    b.   date and time a user logged in and out;

    c.   terminal accessed (location and asset number);

d.   internet access (dates, times and sites visited);

e.   access to removable media; and

f.   applications accessed.

Audit logs will usually be retained for a period of time (e.g. 90 days) before being automatically deleted, unless saved for investigation purposes. It is important that audit logs are protected from alteration once they have been saved to ensure their integrity as a source of evidence.

Correlation Analysis

This is where separate, but related log information is compared to identify suspicious activity. For example, the access control records for staff entering and leaving the building could be compared to system access records. If an individual logs onto a terminal, but has not entered the building, this may indicate a breach of access control or that someone else has logged-in using their credentials. There are software applications available which can collate logs from different IT systems and analyse them based on a defined set of parameters. They can produce a report of suspicious behaviour which can be investigated further.

Synchronising Data Logs

It is important that different systems are synchronised so that comparisons can be accurately made for correlation analysis and collection and integrity of evidence. For instance, a comparison of access control logs between an AACS and IT system would only be possible if the internal clocks were synchronised to ensure they both recorded the correct time. Audit logs must also record data in a consistent format. For instance, a log for the access control system may only record users by their card number and PIN but not their name. An IT access log may record users by their terminal number. In such instances, the data between the systems will be incomparable. A consistent format should be determined to identify users on different systems, for instance, a user ID or staff number.

Fault Logging

Faults with the IT system should be recorded and retained on record for a period of time (e.g. 90 days) to enable trends to be identified. The remedial action taken to address these faults should also be recorded on the log, including the details of the engineer who carried them out. Fault logging can help identify vulnerabilities in the IT system and malicious activity.

Collection and Integrity of Evidence

Some unauthorised activity on a network may constitute a criminal offence and the organisation may be required to submit information as evidence for a legal process. It is important that information on system misuse is collated and preserved in a form which ensures its integrity and credibility as evidence. Identifying details of evidence (e.g. dates, times, user identity, node addresses) must be accurate. Multi-user logins must not be permitted and users actively prevented from sharing login credentials. Once a potentially illegal act has been identified, information must be preserved in its original form and a chain of custody established to track all those who subsequently had access to it.

Monitoring, Analysis and Reporting

Collecting information on its own is useless. Protective monitoring is only effective if suspicious activity is identified, analysed and reported to someone who can investigate it further. Once the individuals responsible for protective monitoring have identified significant suspicious activity, they should produce a formal report and submit it to the security department, or internal audit department, for investigation.

Further Reading

Cobb.C: Network Security for Dummies (2002); John Wiley and Sons

Gollmann.D: Computer Security (2010); John Wiley and Sons

Goodrick.M and Tamassia.R: Introduction to Computer Security – International Version (2010); Pearson

Kizza.J: Guide to Computer Network Security – Computer Communications and Networks (2013); Springer

McNab.C: Network Security Assessment – Know your Network (2007); O'Reilly Media

Pfleeger.C and Pfleeger.S: Security in Computing (2006); Prentice Hall

Vacca.J: Computer and Information Security Handbook (2013); Morgan Kaufmann;

Wang.S and Ledley.R: Computer Architecture and Security: Fundamentals of Designing Secure Computer Systems (2014); John Wiley and Sons

3.6
Communications Security

The aim of communications security is to prevent unauthorised access or interference to telecommunications systems and the information processed on them.

The objectives are:

    a. **access:** to ensure only authorised users have access to communications systems and the information transmitted on them;

    b. **authenticity:** to ensure the integrity of information processed on communications systems;

    c. **availability:** to ensure communications systems can be accessed, on a continual basis, whenever required.

Examples of specific threats to communications security include:

    a. **interception:** unauthorised access to information on a communications network either to obtain intelligence about the organisation or to falsify information;

b. **traffic flow analysis:** analysing patterns in communications which can reveal valuable intelligence about the organisation;

c. **jamming:** electronically blocking communications between authorised users which is mainly carried out against radio communications systems;

d. **falsification:** generating false communications by unauthorised parties;

e. **compromise of cryptographic material:** loss or theft of cryptographic material; and

f. **loss of communications equipment:** loss or theft of hardware.

Communications systems involve a number of technologies including internet, e-mail or Voice Over Internet Protocol (VOIP), telephone, facsimile and radio. It usually involves electronic communications, therefore, mail would not be included and would usually be covered by document security procedures which are discussed further on.

Interception is the main threat to communications systems and can be used by hostile parties to gain information which could be used to damage the organisation and its business interests. Information could also be altered to confuse or mislead the organisation and inhibit its work. Intercepting communications which are unencrypted is relatively straightforward as the information is instantly accessible to hostile parties. However, if the communications are encrypted, a separate strand of interception is required, known as cryptanalysis. This is the unauthorised decryption of encrypted communications traffic.

Traffic-flow analysis can provide a hostile party with valuable information about the organisation, even if it cannot decipher the organisation's encrypted communications. The more traffic is analysed, the more patterns will emerge. A sudden increase or decrease in traffic-flow can indicate a corresponding increase or decrease in business activity. Rapid, short communications can indicate an incident or emergency. Frequent communications to and from a specific point can indicate a control centre or hub. The times when particular nodes communicate can indicate their role or importance within the organisation.

Jamming can be used to prevent the organisation accessing its communications network in a timely manner. For instance, guard force radios could be jammed to prevent them raising the alarm or coordinating their response, during an attack. Jamming is often a short-term method of attack as its use will usually become known to the target organisation. Therefore, it is often used to aid other forms of attack over a limited period of time.

Falsification can occur when unauthorised persons gain access to a communications network and transmit false or misleading information. For example, an unauthorised member of staff can gain access to communications equipment logged in by an authorised user, but not secured when left unattended. The danger of falsification is that the rest of the security controls around authentication, equipment and transfer may provide credibility to a corrupt message.

The compromise of cryptographic material involves the loss or theft of items used in the encryption and decryption process which will, thereby, compromise all information transmitted using this process. Such items can include encryption keys (either physical or electronic) or key codes. The problem with a loss of such material is the organisation does not know who is now in possession of it. Someone may have stolen it, or found it if was lost, and discarded it without realising its significance. Alternatively, a capable hostile party may have recovered it and be using it to gather sensitive information. The loss or theft of cryptographic material must always be regarded as a compromise of the cryptographic process and remedial action undertaken to reduce the impact of such a loss.

The loss or theft of communications equipment presents a number of risks. The equipment itself may be expensive and will need to be replaced. Some communications equipment may retain a limited volume of data stored on an internal memory which an unauthorised party may be able to recover. The equipment may have an identity code which it displays to other equipment on a network to validate its authenticity. If such a code is not recognised as lost or stolen, authorised users may continue to transmit and receive information unaware that they are communicating with an unauthorised party.

The concept of communications security controls is shown in the diagram in Figure 12: Communications Security Model. The model depicts communications security as three main, interlocking areas: message, equipment and transfer. The message part includes controls to ensure messages are sent from authorised users and are complete and accurate. The equipment part protects the communications hardware and the transfer part protects the information when it is sent.

Fig.12: Communications Security Model

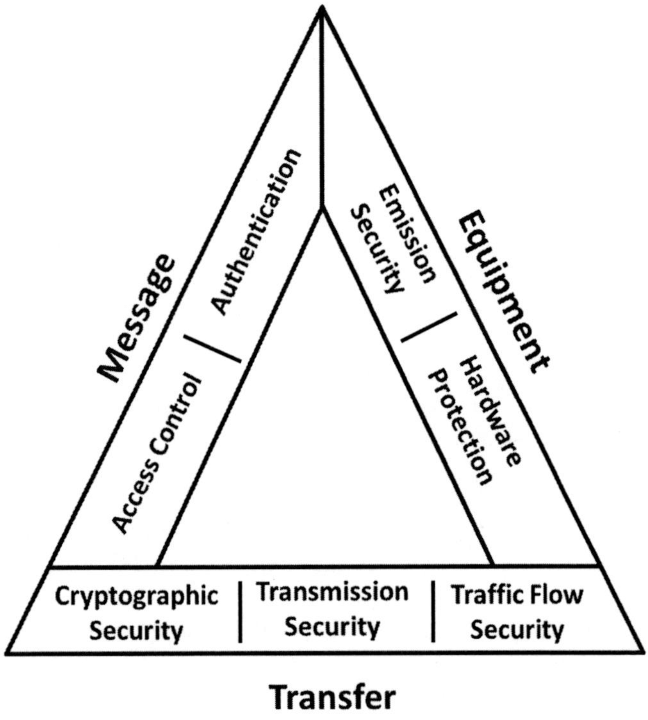

Transfer

Access Control

This describes controls to ensure only authorised persons can access secure communication systems. These controls are very similar to those described in the previous section on IT security.

User Registration

Each user should be authorised by an appropriate person (e.g. a manager or a communications security officer) to use secure communications equipment. The registration process should include a record of the individual's name, the unit they work in, the date they were provided access and the reason access was granted.

Credential Management

Authorised users will require an access credential (e.g. a password, PIN, key or token) to use the equipment. Passwords and PINs should not be written on the equipment, should be changed regularly and not shared with other users. Keys and tokens should be kept secure when not in use, their loss or theft should be reported immediately. Access credentials should be accounted for periodically by carrying out a muster requiring users to check they still have it.

Unattended Equipment

Users should lock-out or log-out of equipment when they have finished using it to prevent access by unauthorised individuals.

Automatic Lock-Out and Log-Out

Equipment which has not been used for a certain period of time should automatically lock-out or log-out in case an authorised user has left it unattended and forgotten to do so.

Review of Access Rights

A user should only retain their access rights for as long as they hold the post in which it was granted. If they move to another post, their access rights should be reviewed to ensure they are still required. Access rights should be audited at least annually to ensure all users retain a business need to use secure communications systems.

Authentication

This describes controls to provide reasonable assurance that a message has been received from the individual who claims to have sent it and that it is complete and unaltered.

Caller ID

Secure communications equipment often displays the name and number of the other party. This should be checked before information is transmitted to ensure the other party is recognised. This can be maintained by a memory stored on the equipment which must be kept up-to-date. Any lost or stolen access credentials should be updated on the equipment's memory to indicate that it has been compromised. If a separate directory of authorised users is held, it should be checked before information is transmitted and should be updated whenever there is a change of user.

ID Challenge

There may be circumstances where an authorised user is suspicious that the party they are communicating with is not who they claim to be. For instance, a security officer's radio may have been lost or stolen or an unauthorised radio used on the network. A caller may contact the control room asking for actions to be undertaken or information to be communicated and may even use a recognised call sign and voice procedure. Another example is a communications system which is accessed at an unusual time or asks for information already successfully transmitted. In such cases, a user can initiate an ID challenge which is where they ask the other party to produce additional authentication. This can be in the form of a code word, or numerical code which they must declare to continue the communications. Sometimes a duress code is also provided to enable the other party to indicate, covertly, that they are being forced to communicate.

Standard Message Format

Messages can be communicated in a standard format to help identify if they have been altered or are incomplete. This can include a header and footer to indicate that the message is complete. The size of the message (e.g. number of pages, lines or words) can be included to indicate if details have been added or removed after the message has been transmitted.

Hardware Protection

This describes controls which prevent unauthorised interference to communications systems hardware. Hardware includes communications equipment and any physical connections between it.

Approved Equipment

The organisation's communication security procedures should clearly state what equipment should be used to process different sensitivity of information. Some information could be processed openly over normal telephone lines or mobile phones. More sensitive information may be restricted for secure communications equipment only. Staff must be briefed on such procedures as part of their induction training and whenever they are provided access to new communications systems.

Appropriate Use

The organisation should establish basic rules on the appropriate use of communications equipment. These should describe what, if any, personal use is permitted and how the equipment should be used and maintained. Rules should also clearly state what constitutes inappropriate use.

Asset Identification

Sensitive communications equipment should be individually identifiable (e.g. a label or stamp with a serial number). The organisation should maintain a register of such equipment including its identification number, any electronic ID it uses to authenticate itself on a network, the location where it is installed and the designated asset owner. Audits should be periodically carried out of such equipment to identify if it has been lost or stolen, but not yet reported. Only sensitive communications equipment (e.g. encrypted telephones or telex machines) will need to be identified and common equipment, such as telephones and fax machines, are usually not included on an asset register.

Asset Protection

Sensitive communications equipment should be protected from unauthorised access. It can be stored in a room where only authorised persons have access or secured to a desk with a retaining cable to prevent it being removed without authorisation.

Cabling Protection

Cabling protection prevents unauthorised access to cabling between communications equipment. Such access can include attempts to intercept communications or simply to sever the cable to prevent use of the communications channel by authorised users. One of the challenges with cabling protection is to ensure it remains accessible for engineers to carry out repairs or modifications, but prevents unauthorised access. Cabling can be secured in robust ducting and locked so that only those with a key can gain easy access. The voltage through wire cabling can also be monitored to detect abnormal fluctuations which could indicate if unauthorised equipment has been attached to it. Different types of cabling are less vulnerable to interception, for instance fibre optic is much more difficult to intercept than copper wire.

Lost or Stolen Equipment

The loss or theft of communications equipment should be reported immediately so it can be blocked on the communications network. Where equipment cannot be blocked, other authorised users must be informed of its loss, so they can check the caller ID to identify equipment which may be operated by a hostile party.

Emission Security

Emissions security or EMSEC describes controls to prevent the unauthorised access to information obtained from the unintentional emanations from communications equipment. This is also known as 'TEMPEST', a US Department of Defence codename referring to the studies it conducted around compromising emissions from electronic equipment (note: TEMPEST is not an acronym). Most electronic devices (e.g. PCs, monitors, printers and communications equipment) emit electromagnetic radiation either directly into the space around the equipment or via a conductive medium such as power lines or communication cables. These emissions may contain data which the equipment is processing at the time. A hostile party could detect such emanations and recover sensitive information.

Reduced Emissions Equipment

Equipment can be purchased which has been designed to emit less electromagnetic radiation. This reduces the risk of emissions being acquired by a hostile party. Information on reduced emissions equipment can be made available by the equipment manufacturer. Older IT equipment usually has greater electromagnetic radiation than more modern equipment, so updating IT hardware will also have a noticeable decrease in electromagnetic radiation.

Electromagnetic Shielding

Equipment can be protected by a metal shield which blocks the electromagnetic radiation. The simplest of these is the 'Faraday cage', named after Michael Faraday who invented it in 1836. It consists of a mesh of copper wire, or perforated metal sheets, which blocks electric fields by channelling electricity through the mesh or sheet. The cage not only prevents electromagnetic emissions getting out, but also prevents harmful electrostatic charges getting in. Shielding can be installed around individual equipment or whole rooms where equipment is located.

Separation of Conductive Material

Equipment can be sited so that it is not close to conductive material, such as other electronic equipment, cabling or wiring. This is sometimes referred to as 'red-black separation'. This can be achieved by installing sensitive equipment in an alcove or designated area of an office with a clear space so equipment is not, inadvertently placed near it.

Cryptographic Security

Cryptographic security describes controls to make information unintelligible to unauthorised parties. Typically, this involves encrypting and decrypting communications, but it also includes other security controls to ensure the confidentiality and integrity of this process.

Figure 13: Encryption-Decryption Process shows the process to encrypt and decrypt a message.

Fig.13: Encryption-Decryption Process

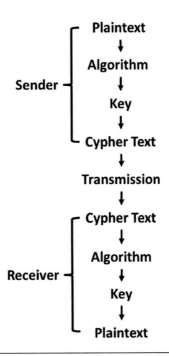

Unencrypted messages are known as 'plaintext', they are encrypted into 'cipher text' by means of an 'algorithm' or 'cipher' (a process for converting a message from plaintext to cipher text) and a key (the unique parameters which tell the algorithm how to convert plaintext to cipher text). When the message is transmitted, the process is repeated in reverse to translate the cipher text back to plaintext.

Algorithms

Algorithms fall into two categories: symmetric and asymmetric. Symmetric key algorithms, also known as private key algorithms, use the same key, shared by both the sender and receiver, to encrypt and decrypt the message. This poses two main vulnerabilities. Firstly, if someone loses the key, both keys must be changed. If there are multiple senders and receivers, all keys must be changed if one is compromised. Secondly, if the same key can encrypt and decrypt a message and that key is compromised, a hostile party can decrypt a message, alter it, and encrypt it again before sending it to the receiver. The receiver may accept the authenticity of the message because it is encrypted without realising it has been altered. Symmetric key algorithms can convert messages from plain text to cipher text in two methods. Block ciphers take a predetermined amount of the message and encrypt it. Stream ciphers encrypt the message each bit at a time. Stream ciphers are commonly used where data is being continually transmitted (e.g. across an IT network) whilst block ciphers are commonly used for communications of a limited, predetermined length. Asymmetric key algorithms, also known as public key algorithms, use two separate keys. A public key, available to all senders, is used to encrypt a message, but it cannot decrypt it. A separate private key, held only by the receiver, is used to decrypt the message. Asymmetric key algorithms often avoid the vulnerabilities associated with symmetric key algorithms.

Hash Functions

A hash function converts data, known as the 'message', into an abbreviated value, known as the 'message digest'. The data cannot be determined using the value and any changes in the data will create a different value. When a message is transmitted, the hash function is applied by the receiver and compared to the hash included in the message. If the two match, the message has not been altered during transmission. Hash functions can be used to verify the integrity and authenticity of a message.

Digital Signatures

Digital signatures are used to identify the sender of a message, prevent the sender from denying they sent it and ensure the message was not altered during transmission. Digital signatures are created by encrypting the hash function using the receiver's public encryption key. The receiver decrypts the message using their private encryption key and checks that the hash included in the message is the same as the one in the digital signature.

Certificates

A certificate is produced by a trusted third party, known as the Certificate Authority (CA), which maintains a record of a sender's identifying details, (e.g. their name, organisation and address) and their public encryption key. A sender transmits a message via the CA which provides a certificate verifying that the public encryption key belongs to that particular sender.

Key Management

A key may be a physical token (e.g. literally a key which is plugged into communications equipment) or an electronic key (e.g. a code entered into communications software). The key is the most important part of the cryptographic process as its loss will compromise the whole process. There are a number of security controls associated with key management, including:

a. **key generation and storage:** an organisation will normally allocate responsibility for overseeing its encryption key management to a designated custodian. They will be responsible for generating new keys, ensuring they are kept secure until they are distributed and ensuring they are distributed securely to authorised users. Keys will normally only be used for a limited period of time before a new key is generated. Keys not yet distributed should be stored securely and access only provided to a limited number of authorised individuals;

b. **key distribution:** a secure method of distributing keys to authorised users must be used. Electronic keys should not be distributed over the network they will be used on because, if the previous key was compromised, so will the next one. The distribution of physical keys will normally be by hand or trusted courier and an audit process used to track the handling of the keys between custodian, courier and receiver. Electronic keys can also be sent manually or on a separate IT system with a comparable (or higher) level of security;

c. **key strength:** the length of an electronic key determines its strength. Key length is measured in bits (segments of data) and the more bits a key has, the stronger it will be. There are accepted industry standards for key length which the organisation should refer to when considering what keys to adopt; and

d. **compromised keys:** physical keys must be audited regularly (e.g. every 12 months). If a key is compromised, it must be changed and existing keys withdrawn and destroyed.

Transmission Security

Transmission security describes controls to prevent unauthorised access to transmissions by means other than cryptanalysis. The objective is to reduce the risk of detection, interception and jamming of communications.

Frequency Hopping and Spread Spectrum

This is where the frequency of radio communications is changed rapidly in a predetermined sequence known to both the transceiver and receiver. This makes the transmission much more difficult to detect and intercept. The transmission can be spread over a much wider frequency range than it would normally require to make it harder to detect.

Anti-Jamming

Jamming can be achieved by transmitting a signal on the same frequency and with the same modulation as the target's receiving equipment, but with a stronger signal strength. Digital signals are more robust to jamming and most modern communication systems will use these. Some communications equipment will also have anti-jamming detection which will alert the operator to such an attack. The most common anti-jamming technique is to change frequencies to an alternate channel known to both the transmitter and receiver. This can either be agreed in advance or communicated via another medium other than radio transmission. Another anti-jamming method is to increase the strength of the signal so that it overpowers the jamming signal.

Traffic-Flow Security

Traffic-flow security describes controls which conceal the presence and volume of traffic on a secure network. If a hostile party intercepted the organisation's communications, it may not be able to read the encrypted traffic, but it may be able to obtain useful information from the flow of communications traffic.

Call Signs

Some organisations may use a radio network to communicate between staff and a central station. For example, security offices often use radios to communicate with a control room. Call signs are a key method of traffic-flow analysis as they identify the nodes in the network and what function they perform. It is common for control rooms or main hubs to use call signs such as 'control' or 'zero' which clearly denotes their role. Sequential call signs are also sometimes used such 'Alpha One' for a team leader, 'Alpha Two' for their deputy and so on. Call signs should be changed periodically and avoid using a hierarchical or sequential structure.

Dummy Traffic

Normal network traffic can be topped-up with false traffic to ensure a continuous volume is always present. This can hide periods of increased or decreased network activity. It can also make cryptanalysis more difficult as the dummy traffic can be unintelligible and a hostile party may not be able to differentiate between it and normal network traffic.

Continuous Encrypted Signal

This is maintained irrespective of whether network traffic is being transmitted. Without decrypting the traffic, it is not possible to distinguish between an empty communications link and one which is transmitting information.

Further Reading

Bauhaus.M, Campagna.R and Iyer.S: Mobile Device Security For Dummies (2011); John Wiley and Sons

Chen.L and Gong.G: Communications System Security (2012); Chapman and Hall

Ferguson.N, Schneier.B and Kohno.T: Cryptography Engineering – Design Principles and Practical Application (2010); John Wiley and Sons

Hoffman.D: Blackjacking – Security Threats to BlackBerry Devices, PDAs and Cell Phones in the Enterprise (2007); John Wiley and Sons

Huner.G: Mobile Phones and Portable Devices Security (2011); Amazon Media

Katz.J and Lindell.Y: Introduction to Modern Cryptography – Principles and Protocols (2007); Chapman and Hall

Park.P: Voice Over IP Security (2008); Cisco Press

Porter.T, Zmolek.A and Kanclirz.J: Practical VoIP Security (2006); Syngress

3.7
Document Security

The aim of document security is to prevent unauthorised access, alteration, dissemination or destruction of sensitive documents.

Its objectives are:

    a. **identity:** to ensure documentation is clearly identifiable;

    b. **access:** to ensure documentation is available only to those with a legitimate business purpose;

    c. **integrity:** to maintain the accuracy, completeness and credibility of documentation; and

    d. **audit:** to ensure documentation is regularly accounted for and reviewed.

Examples of specific threats to document security include:

    a. **loss or theft:** the unauthorised release of documentation outside a controlled environment;

b. **unauthorised disclosure:** the release of contents of a document to unauthorised persons;

c. **misdirection:** documents being diverted, intentionally or inadvertently, to unauthorised persons;

d. **falsification:** the improper creation or alteration of a document; and

e. **recovery and reconstitution:** the recovery of a document after it has been disposed of and reassembly after it has been destroyed.

Loss or theft of documentation is the most common risk, particularly in public places such as public transport, restaurants or coffee bars where briefcases are left behind or stolen. The biggest problem for the organisation is the uncertainty of where the documentation is and who has access to it. A thief may have taken it and, having found nothing of value to them, thrown it away. It could, however, have been sold to a rival organisation, a pressure group or criminals. Even if someone offers to return the documentation claiming to have found it, it may not be clear whether it has been copied.

Unauthorised disclosure of documentation occurs when an unauthorised individual has access to it, but does not necessarily have possession. An example is a member of staff reading a sensitive document on a train and a curious onlooker reading over their shoulder. Unauthorised disclosure is much harder to detect than loss or theft of a document and it may not be apparent that a breach of security has occurred.

Misdirection occurs when documents are sent to someone other than the intended recipient. Examples include mail sent to the wrong address either by errors in the delivery system or by an incomplete or inaccurate address. E-mails and faxes can also be misdirected, for example, if a previously authorised recipient no longer requires access to them but is left on the distribution list. Faxed documents are particularly at risk because it is easy to mistype a fax number which may result in the document being sent to a completely wrong fax machine. In comparison, mistyped e-mail addresses are often undeliverable and misspelt mail can still be delivered to the correct address. Misdirection can also be intentional, for example, by admin or mail room staff placing a letter in another envelope addressed to themselves or an accomplice. The unauthorised recipient can open the letter, copy the contents before repackaging it and sending it to its intended address.

Falsification of documents includes forging signatures, altering details (e.g. dates, quantities, costs and delivery addresses) and forging an entire document (e.g. a permit or purchase order). Falsification can be carried out by insiders seeking to extend their access to assets, to hide a misdemeanour or to incriminate colleagues with whom they have a grievance. External parties can also falsify an organisation's documents to cause embarrassment, implicate them in illegal or unethical acts or to carry out fraud.

Recovery and reconstitution occurs when documents which have been disposed of are removed from the waste. A simple example is someone removing documents from a waste paper bin which the owner has carelessly discarded. An organisation's rubbish bins could also be searched to identify documents which have been disposed of in what is colloquially known as 'garbology' or 'dumpster diving'. The reconstitution of documentation involves reassembling a document which has been destroyed. For example, by sticking shredded pages back together. This is becoming more difficult as shredders improve and even the most basic models are now 'cross-cut' which cuts the paper into short, confetti-like pieces making reconstitution much harder.

The concept of document security is shown in Figure 14: Document Security Model.

Fig.14: Document Security Model

The model depicts the various stages in the life of a document, moving clockwise, from its creation, through various stages of its handling, to its destruction. The number of stages will depend on the sensitivity of the document. Not all documents will follow all the stages and the extent of security controls will be defined by its sensitivity.

Document Creation

Document creation ensures that documents can only be produced by appropriate individuals and security controls are applied immediately as soon as the document is made. When documents are informally made, they can evolve from a few ideas in a notebook which are eventually copied into a formal report. In the intervening period, appropriate security controls may not be consistently applied and only the author may be aware the document exists because it has not yet been recorded on a document register. A formal document creation process ensures that all documents, including those in draft, can be identified and are protected from unauthorised access from the moment they are produced. Document creation controls include:

a. **limited hard copy documents:** forms can be produced electronically which provides greater control over them. Hard copy forms should be limited to circumstances where they are absolutely necessary;

b. **registration:** whenever a member of staff wishes to set up a new electronic document, they must enter details on a registration form which will automatically allocate a unique reference number;

c. **standard document templates:** a uniform set of templates for creating letters, memos or reports can include fields for security related information such as the security classification, author, version control and a registry reference; and

d. **authorised access to templates:** some standard document templates need only be accessible to specific staff. For example, purchase orders may only be accessible to staff authorised to purchase goods or services. Restricting access to such documents limits the scope for misuse.

Document Owner

An identifiable individual should be given specific responsibilities for a document, or collection of documents. In some cases, the owner of a document is obvious and unambiguous as one person has produced it for another, as in the case of a letter. The letter is owned by the author until it is sent to the recipient, whereupon they become the owner and the author retains a copy. In this example, there are only two copies of the letter, each owned by individuals clearly identified in it. However, a file may be deposited in the organisation's registry, containing a number of documents completed by different individuals, which can be checked out by any number of staff. The registry manager may not have a full understanding of the contents of the file, or its sensitivity, and may not be able to make decisions on who should receive it and how they should use it. Therefore, it is necessary that a document owner be nominated who is familiar with the topic of the file, even if they are not fully aware of its contents, so they can provide advice to the registry manager on how it should be handled. Document owners should be of an appropriate seniority and familiar with the subject matter and its sensitivity. They should also be reasonably accessible so they can respond to questions about the document.

It is often impractical for the document owner to process the document themselves (e.g. copying, distributing, filing, auditing and destruction) and a document officer can be appointed to carry out these functions on the document owner's behalf. The document officer is often a junior member of staff and they do not require a detailed knowledge of the subject matter as the owner. They do require a good knowledge of the organisation's document handling procedures and have easy access to the owner to refer to, if required.

Identification and Marking

Document identification and marking is a range of controls to ensure documentation is individually identifiable with sufficient detail to enable it to be appropriately processed and protected.

Basic identification markings include:

    a. the author;

    b. the document owner, if different from the author;

    c. the date and time the document was produced;

    d. the version of the document, if it is subject to amendment;

    e. a unique reference number;

    f. the copy number of the document, if a number of copies are made;

g. the page number and total number of pages;

h. the organisation's name and address; and

i. the recipient's name and address.

Documents can also be marked to indicate their sensitivity. The most common security identifier is 'Personal and Confidential'. A scale can also be used to identify the security classification of documentation. Governments use such systems and mark their documents with descriptors such as 'SECRET' and 'TOP SECRET'. An example of a simple security classification system is a 'traffic light' model using coloured flags in the top right hand corner of the document. The flag should have its colour printed on it to ensure it is still identifiable if copied on a black and white photocopier or fax machine:

a. **Red:** the document must only be made available to those recorded on its distribution list. Further distribution is only permissible with the prior written permission of the author or owner. The document must be kept locked away when the holder is away from the office and must be destroyed securely;

b. **Amber:** the document may be circulated freely within the organisation but not communicated outside it unless prior approval has been obtained from the author or owner. The document may be left on desks during the day but must be locked away at night and destroyed securely when no longer required; and

c. **Green:** the document may be circulated freely outside the organisation, provided it is in its original form. Any amendments must be agreed in advance by the author or owner. The document does not have to be locked away at any time and does not need to be destroyed securely.

In this example, the system is easy for staff to remember but it would not be immediately obvious to an outsider the sensitivity of the document if they happened to oversee it.

Unique Material

Documents are more difficult to falsify if they are printed on unique material with security features built into them or applied after the document is completed. Examples of security features include watermarks, holograms, foils, laminate coatings and embossed stamps.

Such measures are only effective if supplies of blank materials are protected from unauthorised access and made available only to a limited number of people. The security of such material can be enhanced if the design changes frequently to ensure that, if any blank material has been misappropriated, it will only be usable for a limited time. It is important that recipients of such documents are informed of the security features they contain so they are able to identify a forgery.

Validation

Sometimes documents can be produced by a number of people within the organisation, or even its customers, but require validation by an authorised person. This avoids burdening an individual with the laborious task of producing large quantities of documents themselves, but ensures documents are only approved by someone with appropriate authority.

Validations can be indicated on a document by a number of methods, including:

a. a unique reference number, which could be verified by a register held by the authorised person;

b. an authorisation stamp; and

c. a signature of the authorised person.

It is important to protect the method of validation from unauthorised use. A register of validation numbers should only be added or amended by a limited number of appropriate individuals and an authorisation stamp should be kept secure when not in use. Signatures can be verified using an authorised signatory list.

Document Register

A document register records details of documentation to ensure it can be accounted for. The register is completed when the document is produced and includes details such as:

a. title, reference number and the latest version number;

b. number of pages;

c. the author and owner (if different);

d. the recipient;

e. security marking;

f. retention period; and

g. a brief summary of the document.

Small organisations may have only one document register held by a Head of Registry or other appropriate person which will include all documents produced and received. Larger organisations may have separate registers for different business units which will be the responsibility of nominated persons within each unit. Registers can be in hard copy, but it is also common for them to be electronic to enable them to be accessed by authorised persons at different locations and searched quicker and easier.

Tracking

Documents can be tagged or marked to enable them to be electronically tracked. Such markings can include a barcode, magnetic strip or a Quick Reference (QR) tag. An electronic reader can be used to scan these marks which will access the document record for the operator to view and amend. Document tracking can be used to identify files containing numerous documents or individual documents themselves, such as purchase orders, application forms or requisition forms. The advantages of document tracking include:

a. to enable documents to be followed through a process involving different parts of the organisation and its contractors;

b. to enable large quantities to be audited quickly and accurately; and

c. to produce a log describing the history of a document including when it was created, who had access to it, what additions or revisions were made during its life and when it was destroyed.

Of course, it may not be practical to track every document the organisation produces or receives and a list of appropriate documents may be established which require tracking.

Access and Authentication

Documents must only be provided to those who are authorised to receive them. In many cases the distribution list will help ensure this. However, it is not always possible to foresee all occasions when an individual has a legitimate need for a particular document and requests for new copies will always arise. This is where access and authentication is necessary. It is a very old trick by journalists, information brokers and protest groups to contact an individual, state that they are from another part of the organisation and ask for a document to be faxed to them. By quoting the correct title of a genuine business unit within the organisation, or even a name of an individual that works there, these requests may seem plausible. A professional telephone voice and a little charm will do the rest. People naturally want to be helpful and will also be inclined to respond to such requests quickly to avoid the person calling back. One method of authenticating such requests is to ask the individual to send an e-mail describing what document they require and why they need it. The e-mail address will confirm where they come from, and the request can be checked with the document owner before it is actioned. The e-mail can also be retained for audit purposes. If the individual is not able to send an e-mail, caution should be exercised before a document is sent by fax. The fax number should be checked against the organisation's contact directory and, if it cannot be found, the request should be declined. Requests for documents should not be sent to personal e-mail accounts.

Storage

Documents must be stored in a manner appropriate to their sensitivity. It is often impractical to store documents in a basement vault as staff may require regular, convenient access to them. If access is time consuming and inconvenient, staff will find alternative arrangements to keep documents they are currently using. Some organisations have secure file stores on each floor, or each open-planned office where documents can be locked at the end of the day. Steel filing cabinets with appropriate locks can also be used and have the added advantage of being small enough to keep close to the desk of staff using them. Desk pedestals are relatively easy to force open or remove from the premises and should only be used for non-sensitive documents.

The storage of documents outside the organisation's premises should also be afforded appropriate protection. Staff who work from home should have secure storage, which other family members do not have access to. Staff working at other locations (e.g. events and meetings where they need to store document in cars or hotel rooms) could be provided with portable storage units. Lockable steel chests can be tethered to the luggage straps in the boot of cars used to transport documents. Document bags made from slash resistant material or with metal link linings can be tethered to a radiator or the bathroom sink in hotel rooms using a steel cable and padlock.

Carriage and Transmission

Documents can be distributed in hard copy (carriage) or electronically (transmission). The method of distribution should be secure to prevent documents being lost, misdirected or stolen. Options for carriage include first class mail, special delivery, recorded delivery or courier. Each option has an increasing cost which must be weighed against the sensitivity and value of the documentation being distributed. Electronic transmission is quicker, can be more secure, and easier to establish an audit trail. However, e-mailed documents are easier to distribute to individuals beyond those authorised to have access to them. This is a particular vulnerability when there are numerous attachments to an e-mail, only one of which is sensitive, and the recipient may not realise this when they forward it to colleagues not included on the original distribution.

Distribution Lists

A distribution list describes the individuals who are permitted access to a document, or collection of documents. It ensures documents are sent only to those with a legitimate business need to receive them and helps identify which individual was responsible for a document which is recovered after it was lost or stolen. It includes details such as:

a. the title and reference number;

b. the security marking; and

c. the copy number of each document and the name and position of the individual who received it.

The distribution list would normally be used by the person distributing the document, either in hard copy or electronically, and would then be filed with the original copy.

Retention

Some documents must be kept for a minimum period of time (e.g. tax records). It is important to ensure that retention dates are specified for records which must be kept for specific periods. Such periods can be defined by law, by regulatory bodies which oversee the organisation's work or by the organisation itself. These retention periods should be determined when the document is created and reviewed during regular audits.

Audit and Review

Audit and review are separate processes. The first to ensure documents can be accounted for and have been processed correctly and the second to consider whether their further retention is required. The auditor will usually be someone who has no involvement in the document process itself. Document registries can be very large and it is not always practical for an auditor to check every record to ensure it is still where it should be and has been processed correctly. The document officer will usually locate every record and compare it to the document register. They will then provide a declaration to the auditor stating that all records are accounted for and have been processed correctly. The auditor will usually select a random sample of records to examine and may also interview the document officer to confirm their understanding of the document handling process.

The review process provides an opportunity to reconsider the retention date and determine if this should be amended. It may be that the document is due for destruction but contains information that is subject to a legal process or an internal review and should, therefore, be retained until these are complete. The reviewer may decide that the original retention period was excessive and the documents could be destroyed sooner. Whatever decision the reviewer takes, they should follow established guidelines to ensure consistency of approach and should also record their decision in the document register.

Destruction

Once a document is no longer required it should be destroyed. A security classification system will help define how different documents should be destroyed. Secure destruction can either be done by the organisation itself or by a contractor which specialises in this field. There are several methods of secure destruction including incineration, shredding and pulping. Copies of documents can be destroyed by the holder after they have exceeded their retention periods. Original copies should follow a process including:

a. authorisation should be obtained from the document owner or authority, preferably in writing by completing a form;

b. the document register should be updated to show that the document has been destroyed;

c. a destruction certificate should be produced which confirms that it has been securely destroyed. It is common for a certificate to cover a range of documents listed on a schedule.

Summary

Security controls form part of the risk reduction element of a risk management process, as described in Section 1. They can be complex and resource intensive to establish and maintain and it is a common error for an organisation to apply as many as possible to all areas of its work. This is done in the belief that each control is sensible and achievable and together will provide the best protection for the organisation's assets. However, over time, this approach is often revealed to be excessively onerous on business operations, fatiguing on staff, and disproportionately expensive. Therefore, it is important that organisations consider carefully what security controls their risk assessment indicates are necessary, what impact they will have on staff and business operations and how practical they will be to maintain over time.

It is more effective for an organisation to have fewer security controls which are consistently and accurately applied than to have many security controls which staff regularly disregard or find ways of working around them. Organisations may also find it easier to implement a minimal number of core security controls and add additional ones over time, if required, rather than introducing them all at once.

It is also an important point that each security field – physical, personnel, personal, information, IT, communications and document – must have comparable and commensurate security controls with each other. This ensures the overall security regime is effective. It is sometimes found that security fields (e.g. physical security) have been increased over time to cope with frequent types of attack (e.g. criminal damage) and other security fields (e.g. personnel security) are neglected. This provides an attacker with the option of changing their method of attack (e.g. obtaining employment with the organisation to get a pass through its physical security controls) when security controls in one specific field become too difficult for the attacker to overcome.

There are three main principles for an organisation to consider when determining its security controls:

    a.   ensure they are proportionate to the risks;

    b.   ensure they are sustainable over time; and

    c.   ensure they are consistent between different security fields.

Further Reading

Blair.B: Safeguarding Critical e-Documents: Implementing a Program for Securing Confidential Information Assets (2012); John Wiley and Sons

Koppenhaver.K: Forensic Document Examination: Principles and Practice (2007); Humana Press

Mendell.R: Document Security – Protecting Physical and Electronic Content (2007); Charles C Thomas Publishing Ltd

Nickell.J: Detecting Forgery: Forensic Investigation of Documents (2007); University Press of Kentucky

Richardson.B: Records Management For Dummies (2012); John Wiley and Sons

Robitaille.D: Document Control : A Simple Guide for Managing Documentation (2005); Paton Press

Shepherd.E and Yeo.G: Managing Records: A Handbook of Principles and Practice (2003); Facet Publishing

Tchao.J: Document Control Recommended Practice: A guide for implementation and audit purposes (2014); Consepsys Limited

Conclusion

The introduction to this book stated that security is more of an art than a science. Whilst it has some consistent methods and concepts, it also requires judgement and perspective to be effective when translated from theory into practice. This is because security is a reflection of the organisation it is operating within, including its unique risks, business practices, attitudes, priorities, outlooks and working culture. Sometimes, even experienced security managers join a new organisation and attempt to transfer the security regime from their last employer to their new one. Students of security courses can also enter their first security job and attempt to bring all that they have learned into their new environment. Both will experience difficulties.

Before attempting to apply any of the concepts or principles described in this book to a practical security role, the practitioner should first understand the organisation and its specific security requirements. They should also develop their knowledge of its current security processes and how they have evolved. A particular security protocol may at first seem inefficient or inappropriate, but further examination into its background may reveal why it exists it its current form.

The effectiveness of a security control will owe as much to how well it is implemented and maintained as the value of the control itself. It is better to retain a risk for a short period of time whilst an effective implementation plan is developed than to rush a control into effect and have it undermined by poor understanding from those required to apply it.

For the security professional, continual education and awareness are vital in maintaining the currency of their skills and knowledge. Security fields are constantly developing in terms of concepts, industry standards and technology. The security professional has a career-long responsibility for learning new techniques, keeping up-to-date with developments in security systems and maintaining awareness of evolving threats.

Glossary

ACL   Access Control List – a list of individuals authorised to have access to specific assets, such as data or applications, on an IT network.

AACS   Automated Access Control Systems – computer system which identifies authorised persons and enables them access through a control point.

AMD   Archway Metal Detector – equipment designed to detect metal passing through a magnetic field generated within an archway, through which an individual passes. Also known as Walk-Through Metal Detector.

CCTV   Closed Circuit Television – a network of one or more cameras which broadcast images to a specific location.

COMSEC   Communications Security – field of security relating to the protection of communications systems and the information processed on them.

CP   Control Point or Check Point – a designated location where security controls are applied to something (e.g. people, vehicles or objects) entering or leaving a controlled area.

CPO   Close Protection Officer – an individual trained to provide protection to persons at risk of physical attack.

CPT   Close Protection Team – a group of CPOs working together to protect an individual or group of individuals.

DDOS   Distributed Denial of Service – a form of electronic attack, mounted from a number of sources, which prevents access to IT systems and data.

DMZ   De-Militarised Zone – a combination of security controls at the boundary of an IT network which typically include an internal and external firewall either side of a server. The server is usually restricted to a function that requires external access.

DoS   Denial of Service – a form of electronic attack which prevents access to IT systems and data.

EA   Electronic Attack – any malicious attack on computer systems using electronic means.

EMSEC   Emissions Security – field of security
             relating to the protection of unintentional
             emissions from electronic equipment.

ICT   Information and Communications
             Technology – electronic systems which
             process information.

IDS   Intruder Detection System – alarm
             system which detects unauthorised
             access to premises.

INFOSEC   Information Security – field of security
             related to the protection of information
             and the systems which process it.
             Usually an umbrella term of the fields of
             IT security, communications security and
             document security.

IPR   Intellectual Property Rights – legally
             recognised rights to a variety of
             intangible assets, such as discoveries,
             inventions and designs.

ITSEC   Information Technology Security – field
             of security relating to the protection of
             computer systems and the information
             processed on them.

PAB   Personal Alarm Button (also known as
             Panic Alarm Button) – a switch which
             activates an alarm to indicate an
             individual's personal safety is at risk.

PBA   Pre-Boot Authentication – requirement
             for an authorised user to enter their log-

in details on an IT system before it begins its start-up sequence.

PIDS
Perimeter Intruder Detection System – alarm system which detects unauthorised access through an external boundary.

PIN
Personal Identification Number – a unique number allocated to an individual to identify them on an electronic system

PIR
Passive Infra-Red – method of detecting unauthorised access through changes in the infra-red spectrum caused by body heat.

POA
Power-On Authentication – see PBA.

SCIF
Secure Compartmentalised Information Facility – an area, separate from other facilities, designated for the secure handling of sensitive information.

SRO
Senior Risk Owner – an individual within an organisation with overall responsibility for managing the risks to its assets and operations.

SSO
Single Sign-On – where an authorised user of an IT system only needs to enter their user name and password once to gain access to all services and applications on the IT system.

TEMPEST
United States of America, Department of Defence code word for the study of the

risk posed by electronic emissions from electronic equipment (note: it is not an acronym).

TNA — Training Needs Analysis – an assessment of what skills are required by different individuals and how these skills will be provided.

UPS — Uninterrupted Power Supply – a system which ensures the continual supply of electrical power to facilities and equipment.

VCP — Vehicle Control Point or Vehicle Check Point – control point where security controls are applied specifically to vehicles.

VMD — Video Motion Detection – method of intrusion detection which uses CCTV cameras to detect movement across its field of view.

VP — Vulnerable Point – a location or area where a specific vulnerability has been identified.

WTMD — See AMD.

Index